The Accidental Real Estate Millionaire

Roy Cleeves

The Accidental Real Estate Millionaire

Copyright ©2020 by Roy Cleeves

All rights reserved.

No part of this publication may be reproduced, stored in a retrieval system, or transmitted in any form by any means—electronic, mechanical, photocopy, recording, or any other—without the prior permission of the author and editor.

ISBN- 978-1-64970-115-2

Printed in Canada

Dedication

This book is dedicated to my late father, Melvin Cleeves, who passed away at the young age of 70 from an unexpected and inoperable cancer.

Mel, as he enjoyed being called, was a wonderfully supportive father who taught me so many powerful life strategies. He taught me to be true to myself, and to not worry even in the worst of times— he would say, "just focus on what you can do to make things better." Some of his best advice that I still practice today is, "have fun and play games often, especially cards and family board games."

My dad also taught me to always respect women and would often say, "If you have a Happy Wife, then you have a Happy Life!"

Mel led by example. He would teach me even when he didn't know he was teaching me. One of the top things he showed me was that we can always do more than we think is possible, including everything from building our own carport together to opening my own business. I am the man I am today because of his support and his love for us and for life.

Thank you, Dad!

- Roy Cleeves

Table Of Contents

Dedication iii

Foreword By Thomas Wong vii

Introduction xi

Chapter One 1

   Part One: The Young Wheeler & Dealer 1

   Part Two: Gut Values 2

Chapter Two: Growing Up Lucky 5

   Part One: Discovering My Strengths 5

   Part Two: Finding My Partner For Life 6

   Part Three: Our First Investment 8

Chapter Three: Never Leave A Man Behind 13

   Part One: Leaving General Motors & Gaining Retail Experience 13

   Part Two: Meeting My Future Business Partner 14

   Part Three: Opening My First Business 15

   Part Four: Getting Into Real Estate 16

Chapter Four: Keller Williams Realty 23

Chapter Five: Building My Team 29

Chapter Six: Family First 37

Chapter Seven: Mindset 41

Chapter Eight: Inspiration 47

Chapter Nine: Dancing With Lady Luck 53

Chapter Ten: Good Versus Great 59

Chapter Eleven: Don't Be Afraid to Just Ask 71

Chapter Twelve: Evolution: My Advice to The Next Generation ... 77

Chapter Thirteen: More Lessons in Real Estate 81

Chapter Fourteen: The Best is Yet to Come 89

Chapter Fifteen: Afterthoughts 93

Epilogue 95

Acknowledgments 99

Special Thanks 99

Author's Bio 101

Editor's Bio 105

Resources 107

Foreword

Thomas Wong

Roy Cleeves, *The Accidental Real Estate Millionaire*, what an incredible story he has to share!

When Roy asked me to be a part of this book by writing the Foreword, of course, I said, "yes!" Roy Cleeves is a great friend and business partner of mine. I'm well aware of what he has accomplished in the real estate industry. Let me tell you, his value is remarkable.

You will find out later in this book, one of Roy's business partners lived next door to my partners. Our business relationship was able to expand in a unique way because it was Roy and his partner, who helped me sell my parents' house. I observed their willingness to walk the extra mile to help to complete the sale. Also, their professional attitude throughout the process became the foundation of our long-term friendship. Roy and I have now been working together on joint venture real estate projects for over 15 years. These days, most people do not stay in a marriage for that long, let alone a business partnership. We faced many challenges together. Even though, at times, we have different opinions, we are always able to work things out and find a solution for any situation.

Finding business partners that you can trust and work with is precious. I have performed many real estate joint ventures with many different people. Although some people only look out for their own best interests and others might have too many opinions on minor issues, Roy is a real team player, and I know he always has my back.

Roy Cleeves is one of the members of my power team! There are many Real Estate Agents and brokers around us, and I have experience with hundreds of them. Roy is one of the major success stories that I have witnessed; some may say that his success is based on luck, but there is more to it than that.

There is an old saying, "Luck favours the prepared!" Would you like to know how Roy became a prepared person? Read this book. You will learn a lot from his life story. It's an enjoyable way to learn and grow rich vicariously through his experiences.

Preparation is not the only ingredient that brought Roy to where he is today. We have another saying, "Luck is when opportunity meets preparation plus action." Over the years, I brainstormed the rent-to-own strategy with many investors. I also encountered many investors who put a considerable sum of money in attending seminars. I couldn't understand how some of them would squander more money on workshops than they invest in real projects. In Roy's book, he shares how he takes strategy and gets results. He acknowledges the investors and friends that have helped him implement his strategies to reach millionaire status.

Great strategy plus action leads to great results!

A positive attitude is contagious. Roy certainly has that infectious attitude. Want to feel a little bit happier? Pick up the phone, and talk to Roy for a minute. You will not regret it. From one of Jack Canfield's books, I learned the success formula (E+R=O). The idea is that we can choose our own response (R) to any event (E). It will then determine the outcome (O). We have the responsibility to make the right choice to achieve the goal. Learn from Roy and be prepared to be the next real estate millionaire.

Good Luck, and enjoy your journey. Have a super-fantastic day!

Thomas Wong

Introduction

We all experience varying degrees of our own success in life, whether you're in technical jobs, engineering, accounting, medical, the technology sector, the education arena, or sales; success is the product of our individual mindset and how we persevere along the way.

Success can be achieved through a clear vision of what it is you truly want, desire, and your belief in yourself and what you can accomplish.

When Gordon So and my business partner, Michelle Carty, both nudged to write a book, I knew they were right!

Gordon is a long time friend of mine, through Thomas Wong. His vision led the way to bring the *Accidental Real Estate Millionaire* to the forefront. Gordon was determined to make my book happen. His encouragement, along with Michelle's is what brought me to these pages.

Michelle would always say to me, "Roy, You have to get your story out there. You made over sixty deals in your first year in real estate. You've helped many agents get on their feet. It's time to model what you do and share your knowledge with people around the world." These are the comments that allowed me to take a step back and reevaluate myself as a businessman.

During my first year in real estate, I hit the jackpot when I made over sixty deals. I was told that these stats are rare in your first year in real estate, so I knew I was on the right track in the industry.

In this book, I'll share with you my experiences in the world of real estate, from when I got my license to how I got into investing and the partnerships that allowed me to evolve along the way. I'll take you through the art of making a good business deal, how to satisfy your clients, and the right kind of investments that will lead you to financial freedom.

Making my first million was easy yet not fast. In fact, the most challenging part was believing that I could become a millionaire. The next step was formulating a plan that would take me towards all that I was capable of accomplishing. The key was to not only expand on something I enjoyed doing but to master a pathway that suited my skill set.

What you are willing to do or not willing to do will set your direction in life. Allowing people to help you achieve your goals is something that takes trust and a sense of vulnerability. I had to become truly vulnerable in my life to be able to find the courage to make the right moves towards the bigger picture.

This book will also go through the stories of how I built my empire, starting with how I use a positive mindset to sustain success, how I grew from there to becoming the person, the husband, the father, the visionary, and the businessman I am today.

By showing gratitude and asking for help and support when I needed it, I was able to author my own life in a way that brought me happiness and success. I was also able to keep my motivation and vision clear on my way to the top.

The Accidental Real Estate Millionaire has been a long time coming. I'm happy that Gordon So and Michelle Carty convinced me to take the plunge and get my message out there.

Me, Michelle Carty, and Gordon So

As you turn through the pages of this book, I hope you feel joy and inspiration from my struggles and triumphs. Take a journey through the world of real estate as I share my experiences in business, rent-to-owns, and investments. Who knows, maybe you will get the itch to make a new investment in your life, too!

Chapter One

Part One: The Young Wheeler & Dealer

As long as I can remember, I was driven by my love for money. I knew money was essential to have, and I wanted to do what I could to accumulate it!

When I was very young, I was in Tobermory, Ontario, with my family when I saw something glimmering in the water. I was like a magpie, "oh, shiny!"

There it was, bright as the sun's rays, a quarter in the water. As I was mesmerized, staring at it, I began to formulate a plan on how I was going to get it. The water was deep and cold; it was where the ferries came in. I wasn't able to swim at this time, but I was determined to make a move.

The shine of the quarter just drew me in, closer and closer. As I began to reach, I fell in!

Oh boy, was that water cold! As I'm thrashing around, I can hear my sister screaming, "Help, help! He fell in!"

There was a lady who jumped into action to help me. She dove into the water and pulled me out.

As I was freaking out, my sister is freaking out, and we both started running, but I started running in the opposite direction of my sister; away from the cottage. "It's this way; it's this way," she exclaimed.

She ran into the cottage to get our parents. Like a bat out of hell, my dad came and got me. When I got back to the cottage, I felt the warmth of my mother's arms and the fear in her chest. I felt lucky to be alive and finally safe. If that lady didn't pull me out, I would have drowned that day. That was the first near-death experience I had, and it was all for the love of money.

As we drove home, I couldn't get my mind off that quarter. I missed my target this time. Next time, I'd be smarter. I never forgot that day, and my urge for money grew stronger as I became a young man.

Part Two: Gut Values

When I was a teenager, I was always in a rush because most teenagers are. I loved pizza pockets and other fast foods, so I knew we needed a microwave to heat things quickly.

My mom and dad said, "No, it's far too expensive."

Puzzled, I thought to myself, it was only $700 from Sears, and I have some money saved up. I knew I had enough money to buy it, so I decided to approach my mom and dad with a deal.

"Mom and Dad, I will buy the microwave, and I will rent it to you for 50 cents a day if you're okay with that deal."

They said, "Yes, we will do that deal." So, we went to Sears and bought the microwave, and I don't remember what age this was, I do know I was well under 16 years of age because I didn't have my driver's license and microwaves were massive back then.

Over the course of two and a half years, they paid me steadily; this was my first experience of creating a contract. I was hooked. Since that first big purchase, microwaves have drastically reduced in price and size. So, my mom and dad said, "Okay, we're ready to exit the deal. We're going to buy our own microwave, and this is now your microwave."

I was able to get half of the microwave paid for, while using the product myself for that two and a half years before they bought their own, and then, of course, we all used the smaller one. I still used that one when I moved out, that was my first microwave until eventually, I wanted a smaller one.

So there you have it, my first rental was a microwave. At a young age, my focus was on chasing money and creating possibilities. I didn't know this mindset would lead me down the road to success later in life, leading me to become a millionaire.

We all start in this world surrounded by people we look up to and depend on to care for and raise us, along with mentoring us as we grow older to learn that everything has its price. If we work hard for what it is we want in life, we care for it much more than if it was just given to us. The value goes up. My parents always taught me that value, even with simple things like getting a pop to drink from the house. I couldn't just grab a drink out of the fridge. Instead, I would cut the grass, and then I would get the pop!

I understood that everything is worth something, and knowing that from a young age has benefited me in many different ways throughout my life— in the way I do business and how I've learned to make smart investments. In fact, I believe it's one of the reasons I got into investing in properties. I understood the value of each investment I made and used it to create something more out of it, not only for my own benefit but for the benefit of the people around me.

I always think back to my early days, wheeling and dealing, and I'm thankful that my parents directed me to grasp the concept of gut values. It's funny, when you're a kid, you think your parents are out to get you, but in reality, they are out to shape you.

Chapter Two

Growing Up Lucky

Some call it luck; some may call it a series of synchronicities that lead you to the right place. All I can say is; growing up, things happened for me, not to me. Certain events helped me recognize my potential and assisted me in taking action towards what I was meant to be doing throughout my life.

Part One: Discovering My Strengths

I began to recognize the areas where I excelled when I was a teenager. In high school, I was a very social guy. I loved being around people, so naturally, I got involved with different groups around the school. I was on the dance committee. I helped with photography, and I even received a business award for selling ads in the yearbook.

I was never the guy who tried out for sports teams in school; I often found myself skipping gym classes because I just didn't see the point. Where I excelled most was in Math. The patterns, working with numbers, clicked. It just made sense to me.

My advice is to always pay attention to your strengths, rather than harp on your weaknesses. I didn't know it then, but calculating numbers would be a huge part of my life for years to come. It would be a major factor in becoming a millionaire.

Part Two: Finding My Partner For Life

My first job as a teen was at Zellers as a Store Clerk. What motivated me to go after that job was the fact that I was young and needed some way to start making more money. I was determined. Back then, it wasn't easy to find work. Fortunately, I had an uncle who had connections. Zellers, why not? I love sales, and this job did the trick for a teenager, looking to score a paycheque. And I worked at Zellers from when I was 16 right through until I became a student at Wilfrid Laurier University.

Zellers is also where I met my beautiful wife, Nikki, and I'm incredibly grateful for that. I was in my second year of university, and when I began to date Nikki, I was also dating another girl at the same time. It was the early stages of the relationship(s), so I was taking my time going out and getting to know each of the women to see which one was the best fit. The other girl would call me off the hook, and I didn't find it as nearly as attractive as Nikki, who seemed to be a strong, independent woman. Nikki knew how to drive a stick shift Honda Civic, which I found pretty neat since many girls I knew didn't even drive, and if they did, it would not have been a stick shift car. She knew how to make her way around town to get what she needed, self-sufficient to the core, something I admired about her at that time.

I knew Nikki was the one for me as we spent more time together, and I began to realize her spunk for life. She challenged me and kept me on my toes, which I could appreciate. During my time at Zellers and university, our relationship grew into a powerful union. Nikki stood by me as I figured out my path, and it made all the difference having a good woman by my side.

While I was in university, I majored in Business Administration. At the time, I didn't know which direction I was going in with that choice. When Nikki met me, I was interested in banking, yet I did not get any offers or even interviews with banks for a co-op position. My other interest was in sales, and I thought I might enjoy working with cars. So, I applied for a co-op at General Motors and got it!

The co-op position led me to travel all across Canada to different Auto Shows. And it was during this time away from Nikki that I realized just how much I wanted to spend my future with her. When I finished my co-op and my last semester at WLU (Wilfrid Laurier University), my parents planned a large family celebration for my convocation ceremony. At this celebration, I decided to announce my engagement to Nikki, which meant that I had better ask her before that if she would marry me! I picked a nice evening in the Summer of 1985 and got down on one knee while in the basement of my parent's house. I know—not super romantic, yet we were so much in love that it did not need to be a grand gesture. Nikki said yes immediately, and we agreed to make the announcement at the upcoming event.

All of my family and friends attended my convocation, and they were all so proud of me as I was the first one in our family to ever graduate from university. At the same time, I announced our engagement, and the applause grew louder. Everyone loved Nikki, and they were so happy to see that we would be tying the knot. Life was on a solid track.

Shortly after, I was thrilled when General Motors offered me a job in Oshawa, Ontario, at their head office. These were exciting times for a young man. I was learning a lot of new skills, and I was about to start making money doing something I enjoyed. My future was secured with a job set up, even before I graduated. Everything was moving in the right direction!

When I left to move to Oshawa, Nikki came with me, leaving all her family and friends behind in Guelph. This dedication and love made it even clearer to me that Nikki would be my partner for life.

Within one year, General Motors promoted me to the District Manager position in Moncton, New Brunswick. This led to a whole new adventure. I had an excellent education, an awesome job, and an amazing woman by my side. Nikki and I were able to travel and make new friends along the way, and all and all, it was an exciting experience for both of us.

After our venture in New Brunswick, we eventually made our way back to Ontario. Home is where the heart is. And, it was time for Nikki and me to begin to focus on our home lives. In university, we lived separately when we were dating, and that worked in the beginning stages. But as we were becoming young adults, we were ready to start to talk about being committed to one another by having children and creating our own family. When Nikki and I discussed merging our lives for the long run, we agreed that even though at some point, we may be upset or angry with each other that we would never disrespect each other. We also agreed not to ever joke about breaking up. You see, once you joke about something like that, it kicks the door open in your mind that it is possible. It becomes something you think about, and then it becomes something you will do, instead of keeping your all-important relationship together, which is the goal. Our mutual agreement allowed us to realize our values were in sync. We were ready to commit and ready to have kids!

Part Three: Our First Investment

When Nikki moved in with me, she came with a plethora of boxes. Oh, did she ever have a lot of clothes, and we couldn't even unpack all of them; there just wasn't enough space. I would wake up in the middle of the night to go to the washroom, and I stubbed my toe on the boxes. Thinking to myself, "Oh, Nikki!"

The weekend after we moved in together, we had to get out; it was just so crammed with all of our belongings all around the apartment. As we were driving around, we began to look at houses that accidentally caught our eyes. At the time, we didn't even know if we could afford a house. Both of us had a little bit of money saved, but I wasn't sure if it was enough for a big investment, like buying our first house.

We saw an open house in south Oshawa, pulled in the driveway, but didn't realize it was after 4 p.m. As we got out of the car, we were met with a pleasant lady named Janice Money (yes, her name really was Money– see how money shows up in my life?) who was the Real Estate Agent.

Janice asked us, "Are you the two that the office called about who were arriving late?"

We said, "No, but can we come and have a look?"

She replied, "Yeah, of course! Come on in."

As we stepped inside the house, we were overwhelmed with that beautiful hot apple pie and cinnamon fragrance. Instantly, we had a feeling like we were home. As we spoke with Janice and she continued to show us around the space, Nikki and I knew we had to jump at the opportunity presented to us. It didn't take long for us to take a leap of faith. By that Monday night, we were putting an offer in, and it seemed like it all happened by accident.

1. We accidentally drove down that street, just looking around on a Sunday to get out of our apartment. We were not even looking for a house.

2. It was by accident that the Real Estate Agent was still at the house awaiting a late showing that day that (as far as we know) never showed up.

3. Accidentally, we found ourselves putting in an offer on Monday night since we didn't even know if we could buy a house.

4. And it was by accident that I ended up having funds from a Motorcycle accident settlement to have a down payment for this house.

Overall, it just seemed to flow together so quickly.

As first-time buyers, we were excited and nervous at the same time. We may not have known exactly what we were doing, but we were taking a chance and learning along the way. Plus, we just knew we needed to find a home for all of Nikki's clothes!

As we were writing up the offer, we had a few concerns, so we made a condition to have both of our parents view the place with us. Both sets of parents came to Oshawa to see our potential new home. As they all stood in the kitchen with us, I could see they were happy with what they were seeing. "YES!" This place has more than enough space for Nikki's clothes. We bought it!

But we had one problem; still, we had eight months left on our apartment lease. We decided to sublet the apartment so we could move into our new home. Any leftover expenses were taken care of, and we were ready for the next chapter in our lives. We continued to grow stronger as a couple, and after a year of living in our new house, we decided to sell it, making $42,000, which was more money than I was making at General Motors for the whole year. Our first investment was all due to luck (the right place at the right time) and Nicki's clothes!

And for most of my clients now in real estate, owning your own home becomes the first accidental investment that leads you on your first step to becoming a millionaire. You see, all of my clients buy their first house to live in and then realize later that it was one of the best investments of their life.

My wife, Nikki, and I on vacation in Italy (taken at the top of the Castel Sant'Angelo in Rome).

Chapter Three

Never Leave A Man Behind

Part One: Leaving General Motors & Gaining Retail Experience

Through the years, I grew tired of my corporate job at General Motors, and I decided to switch things up! I wanted to get out there and start making more money. When I saw what dealer sales managers were making, I dove into the retail arena.

I worked at Nissan Canada for a while, eventually branching out to Toyota, Canada, before landing on my feet at Erin Park Lexus Toyota in the Retail Sector. Working for dealerships allowed me to expand, but as much as I liked working in cars, I felt as though my journey there was coming to an end. I needed to make a change, and it was time.

Part Two: Meeting My Future Business Partner

I met Michelle Carty in 1996 while working at CDI College together in Hamilton. Our mission back then was to find the right solution for people who were looking to return to school. We did whatever we could to onboard people in the programs to improve their lives and further their education. We often would go to high schools to pitch CDI and put a lot of focus on advertising, which was a great way to draw people in to want to learn more about what CDI had to offer. During my time working with Michelle in the 90s, I developed a bit of a nickname for her. I called her 'the hammer' because she wouldn't take no for an answer. It was back then that I took notice that she was a hardworking woman, with a good business sense. Michelle brought a lot to the table.

Michelle and I had a lot of laughs working together too. She always joked that when she was trying to be serious in the office, I would walk across the room with boxing gloves on, doing everything I could to make her laugh. It's that kind of business relationship that supports a lasting partnership. We made things fun, which more than got us through the stresses of the day.

When Michelle and her husband started a family together, we shared a ride to work every day to make it easier for her while she was pregnant. Michelle soon had her baby, Jovi, and once Michelle was ready to go back to work, Nikki even offered to babysit. As friends and in business, our mindsets complimented one another from the beginning. Together, we began to develop a vision that would later lead to many victories early in our partnership in real estate over the years.

During our time at CDI, our goals enhanced, and eventually, both of us left CDI to take on new ventures in 1998.

Part Three: Opening My First Business

In 1990, our very close friends, Jamie and Heidi Bennett from Kingston, opened four Jumbo Video stores, and they were very successful. I began to itch to open up a business of my own. My entrepreneurial side led the way towards buying into the Jumbo Video franchise.

The first year the business did really well! But in the second year, there was a massive paradigm shift in the industry. People started streaming videos rather than renting video cassettes. I broke even that year, and by the third year (in 2001), I found myself closing the doors.

Although it was a great business model, due to the digital world rise, it was the most extended three years of my life. The store didn't have a chance. I began to realize; sometimes, in life, you have to take a few steps back in order to leap forward!

My first instinct at that time was to call my old friend, Michelle, to tell her what was happening with the Jumbo Video franchise. I thought she might have an idea of what steps I could take to get me out of the hole I was in. I began to explain to her that I wasn't going to go bankrupt, but I was going to be taking a loss. I was shutting down the store and looking for my next move. Where was I going to go from here?

I've always tried to remain a positive guy, but I did hit a turning point after shutting down my Jumbo Video store. Thankfully, I managed to save some of my money, and I had the support to find a new direction. Within a few months, Michelle had got me a job working at Trios College as a Director. I landed on my feet due to remaining positively optimistic and from the help of my dear friend.

Part Four: Getting Into Real Estate

During my time working at Trios, my brother-in-law, Chris Abbott, had invited me to tag along to an information session about a real estate course. I think Chris secretly knew he would not be faced with any resistance from me to tag along with him to the course as I was always open to new opportunities. Real estate caught my interest; I just didn't know exactly how to get involved in it. Through the Whitney Canada course called 'Zero Down,' the road was paved.

This was an exciting time for us, and we decided that we would work together to buy as many homes as we could with no money down.

For our first home, we bought an 80-plus-year-old house at 98 London Road in Guelph, Ontario. It was being used as a student rental, and the tenants were paying so much money that we had our down payment funds back from the rent within two months. And it ran very well until the end of the school year when all of the tenants moved out. Now we were faced with putting in new tenants for which we had no experience or training. That was not part of the real estate course, yet it should have been.

We decided to turn the home into a triplex, which we later found out was not allowed by the City of Guelph as it was only zoned as a duplex. Regardless we now rented out three areas, and unfortunately, I rented out the main floor to a terrible tenant that showed up with cash for the first and last and had a U-haul truck hiding around the corner. It seemed as though many other landlords had rejected him. It only took us a few months to find out why. He stopped paying rent, partied all night, and upset the other tenants. And he eventually fell asleep while cooking chicken wings in oil on the stove, which lead to a kitchen fire.

When Chris and I went to Guelph to get the rent, we found that the house had been burnt up and that the tenants had been threatened by the main floor tenant not to call us. So, this was a terrible surprise. We then learned how to evict a tenant and how to sue for damages in small claims court. We were successful, and yet this was a very stressful time.

We also decided to keep as much of the insurance money as possible by doing the repairs to the triplex on our own with the help of our fathers. Thank you, Mel, and thank you, Bernie Abbott! We worked our day jobs, and at night we would go to the rental property to paint and fix all that we could. Along the way, we decided that we would sell the property, yet wouldn't it be great if we had our real estate license so that we could save on those crazy fees that the REALTOR®'s charge?

Then an important day came. It was the day that Chris called me with excitement in his voice! Chris's exact words on the phone that day were, "Hey buddy; I just signed up for the Ontario REALTORS® course." And before he could even finish the sentence, I had a bold response, "What?" I said, "Well, you're not leaving me behind!"

I think I even hung up on him and raced to call OREA (Ontario Real Estate Association) to sign myself up and ordered my course that same day. There was no way that I was going to miss this opportunity. This moment spurred the memory of when I was eight years old and fell in the lake trying to get that shiny quarter I so desperately wanted. I started laughing as I leaned back in my chair and put my hands on my head, knowing I was making a move that would lead me towards more shiny quarters.

The right people will always help motivate you and build you up to make you feel like you belong, as though you are part of something bigger and better. My brother-in-law Chris was just that guy for me and for that, I thank him.

Chris and I went on to further our education by becoming Real Estate Agents together. I was so scared yet the happiest man alive because here I stood with a license to print money and a new job in commission sales. So, where do I take this? I thought to myself.

I was motivated even more this time to succeed because, after the video store closing, the feeling it had left me with was that I felt as though I wasn't even half a man. I needed to feel whole again. It was vital for me to be able to provide for my family, so I remember saying to myself in my first year, "Okay, Roy, you got this. You can turn this around. Not only for yourself, but for your family and for all that hold you in high regard." I love my parents, but I did not want to eat at their house every night of the week. I knew that I needed to sell one house a month to be able to pay my mortgage to keep the roof over our head and another so that we could buy the basics like our own food.

Roy Singh (yes, another REALTOR® named Roy—we were the only two in the Waterloo region) from Century 21 Home Realty was our REALTOR® when we moved to Kitchener after closing the video store. When I became an investor and decided that I would do the REALTOR® course, I reached out to Roy and asked him if he was hiring. As it turns out, he was, and he was happy to invite me to work at his office.

Century 21 Home Realty worked out well because I knew I needed training and support, and Century 21 was happy to see that I was hungry to make it, so they started to teach me the ropes. I learned how to reach out to people and how to use all of the right tools to communicate with potential clients to work with me, and I became good at it! It came so naturally to me as though it was my second skin. I was a Real Estate Agent, Nikki was so proud of me, so was I.

At Century 21, the office had a sales manager. His name was Ken Kelly. He saw me coming down the hall, so he sat back down, rolled up his sleeves, and as I approached, he said to me, "Okay, let's get to work. It's time to get you trained." I started advertising listings. I didn't have my own listings or even my own ads yet, so Ken allowed me to promote his, and because of Ken and his listings, that led me to make my first deal. And going to open houses, oh man, did I do a lot of open houses. In a lot of ways, I owe him a great deal of gratitude for helping me catapult my career into real estate.

Roy Singh also became a great mentor for me, and I was able to go to him for any help and support I needed. Roy saw that I had a lot to offer and that I was always ready to work. My drive was second to none as I pioneered forward scratching, clawing my way to the top towards my first commission cheque, just so I can make sure we had money to pay for our mortgage, bills, etc.

It's always very humbling and rewarding knowing that you come into people's lives and help them make one of the biggest and most important decisions in their lives and get paid well to do it. Some clients have become some of my closest friends, and in turn, they also became like family. These are some of the best parts of being a Real Estate Agent. In a way, you become their hero. And the longer you are in business, the more clients and referrals you can accumulate. During my first six months, I had terrific success. I had sold 25 homes, which meant at least 50 smiles. Within my first year, I sold more than 60 homes. Those were high numbers, according to my broker.

During my time at C21, Roy Singh also ran a company called Discount Mortgage Canada, and he suggested that I get my Mortgage License so that I could also do mortgages for my clients and collect another fee from the lenders for arranging the mortgage. I figured that the more that I know and the more that I can do for my clients, the more they will want to refer me to friends and family and work with me again as their real estate needs would grow. I was right about this, and for ten years, I was a dual agent—mortgages and real estate.

It was purely by accident that I ended up with a brokerage that also had a mortgage company and simply by those few words from Roy suggesting I get my license, which I did, and that advice improved my business. I remember asking Roy how I could become a millionaire and he took the time to explain about investing in real estate as being the best way, yet I would have to be patient as it was not a 'get rich quick system.' I was so anxious to get rich quick that I told him that would take too long and that I would look for another way. Little did

I know that it really was the best plan and that I should have started on that plan right then and there. Instead, I waited until luck once again pushed me towards investing in real estate.

One day while doing a mortgage and a real estate purchase for a lovely couple named Lynda and Allan, I realized that they could not get approved at that time, yet within one year, they would be totally approved for the purchase. As I wanted to help this lovely couple, I thought, if they are willing to pay me $1200 per month plus utilities for this townhouse, then it would cover all of the costs, and then 12 months from now, we can transfer it into their name. I proposed the offer, and I remember to this day, Lynda said, "Roy, we would be absolutely gobsmacked if you would be willing to do that for us!" And just like that, I was once again a landlord—by accident!

When it came to the 12 months later, Lynda and Allan advised me that they preferred to stay as tenants rather than purchase the unit. I was so happy with them as tenants and now enjoyed being a landlord again, so I quickly agreed. They stayed for another four years or so before they moved out, and this became a great long-term rental for me. The difference in tenants made all of the difference in the world.

Thank you, Lynda and Allan!

All of the people at Century 21 became good friends of mine, so when it was time to move on, it made it that much more difficult. Still, I knew I had to move forward and again, step outside my comfort zone.

I worked at Century 21 until 2006. It was my first stomping ground in the industry. I'll always cherish that, and I'll never forget how I got my start as a REALTOR®. Thanks to my brother-in-law, Chris, my Broker, Roy Singh, and my plans of action towards making things happen—*The Accidental Real Estate Millionaire* was on its way towards a vision that even I didn't see coming until later in the game. Stay tuned!

Chris Abbott (left), Bernie Abbott (middle), and me.

Chapter Four

Keller Williams Realty

In 2006, I joined the Keller Williams Golden Triangle Realty Brokerage, and I'm still a part of the agency today. You may be wondering why I choose to leave the past behind to go to Keller Williams. Well, there are many reasons. In this chapter, I'll take you through those reasons. Because I believe in KW so much, I think it's essential to paint the full picture for you, starting with the history of the owners and the agency to building my team.

In 1986, Gary Keller planned to make Keller Williams so attractive to its workers that once they joined the company, they would not ever want to leave it. Well, his plan worked because, to this day, agents who work for KW feel as though they are incredibly privileged to be there.

The agency was founded in 1983 by two men named Gary Keller and Joe Williams. A nice spin on their names, Keller Williams, was created.

Keller Williams has more agents than any other real estate company in the world, with over one-thousand offices in North America and the only privately held global residential real estate brokerage. They started as a single office based in Austin, Texas, selling only local residential real estate. After a few years in business, Keller Williams expanded, becoming one of the largest single office residential real estate firms in Austin, with 72 licensed agents.

Around the mid-1980s, Keller Williams suffered from the housing bubble (I'll share with you the details of the housing bubble later in my book), so they began to offer profit sharing to existing and potential associates. This way, they could retain agents and help get through the recession. The agency was able to sustain what they built and climb their way to the top of the real estate charts, expanding out of Texas and opening up their business model to franchising.

In 1997, Keller Williams was recognized on the Franchise Gold 100 list by Success Magazine.

As it moved into the next century, Keller Williams became one of the fastest-growing real estate offices, with a nationwide agent count of over 30,000.

In 2007, the company launched Luxury Homes by Keller Williams, a division within the company that focuses on luxury real estate sales. They also started KW Commercial, a division providing commercial real estate associates with specialized technology, marketing tools, and resources, allowing agents to keep more commission splits and their profit sharing.

By the 2010s, Keller Williams went international, launching Keller Williams Worldwide as a subdivision. And as of 2014, it is the largest real estate franchise by agent count in North America. They are also the only privately held global residential real estate brokerages in the world.

The competition for Keller Williams Realty is REMAX/Coldwell Banker, HSA, and my old stomping grounds, Century 21 Realty. Keller Williams has well surpassed all of these companies in the volume of transactions by billions. The company's 2017 figures show that their value is at three-hundred billion dollars, which is incredible! They also made it to 'The Thousand' in 2017. 'The Thousand' is a list that comes out once a year in North America. The list only names the most successful real estate companies and their agents. It's an honour to have a team from your company listed, but in 2017, KW had eighty-nine off their teams make it on the list. They were also on the Real Trends 500 list of top brokerages. They had the most market centres of any brokerage firm in the world, with a total of 161.

Another recognition that Keller Williams has received is an acknowledgment by Career Bliss as being one of the "happiest companies to work for." This speaks volumes of their company culture; later in this book, I'll go more into details about the culture at KW because it is a crucial aspect in this day and age, and my team would agree.

Keller Williams is a training company, and because of that, they have endless opportunities for staff. It doesn't matter what your skill-set is or how you learn new information; the strategy is to make everyone feel meaningful and happy at work. Knowledgeable and well-trained staff turned into high-performance teams, translating to success for everyone. Profit-sharing also gave everyone involved some ownership in the company, which is hard to beat!

In 2015, Keller Williams Realty was named the #1 Training company by Training Magazine, not only in real estate, across all industries. And there have been continuously numerous awards for Keller Williams Realty for their training to this day. The training that I received from Keller Williams definitely helped me refine my business and think bigger!

Keller Williams has invested a lot in the latest technology to enhance client services. There are so many new technical avenues available in the real estate market. They aren't cheap, and it takes an investment to implement. Still, they make the most of what is possible in today's day and age, getting answers to questions immediately equals happier clients and more efficient teams.

In 2017, KW Labs was launched, which is a division of the company process devoted to the building and testing of the technology, in addition to KW Keller Cloud. It also introduced 'Kelle,' an app which is referred to as Siri, but for real estate, they use it as a virtual assistant, and an agent-to-agent referral tools platform called 'Referrals.'

KW fosters an environment of caring, which can be rare in the business world. They stand as a model of success for entrepreneurs as well. Both Gary and Joe were visionaries. They started the business with one office and believed that they would turn it into something bigger and better. Within a few years, they had achieved success and continued to expand beyond the norm.

Keller Williams became the number one franchise in the United States by sales volume in 2017, ranking number one in agents and units sold in 2017. Profit-sharing has exceeded $1 Billion, which is one of the most remarkable aspects of the Keller Williams Real Estate company. Since they first began offering profit sharing, they have distributed over a billion dollars to their associates. The estimates for the 2017 year show that this year alone, associates were given $174 million in profit-sharing dividends for the preceding four years. What a great place to work! Most of us would be extremely happy with that kind of profit sharing.

Keller Williams owes their number one spot to John Davis.

John was the team leader who knew how to get things done. When Keller Williams hit critically amid a downturn, their numbers dwindled to 75,000 agents. They turned to a team within the company that was consistently performing at high levels when others were failing. They found one common thread. The highest performers were following the business models created by John Davis. Keller Williams implemented this company-wide, and in a short period, they were back on top and moved into the number one position in the real estate industry not only in America but in the entire world.

Keller Williams continues to grow around the world. They are an excellent company to be a part of, and I highly recommend them to anyone looking to get into real estate.

Chapter Five

Building My Team

I have always preferred to work with others rather than alone. I like to be around like-minded people who have the ability to think bigger.

When I started at Keller Williams, I had a team of only four of us. I thought I would need a smaller office. But Jim Reitzel, who was a broker, said to me: "We are giving you 1200 square feet of space."

I said to Jim, "That's a lot of space for four people. We don't need that much room." He said, "No, it's not. Your team is going to grow, and you're going to need it."

Jim was right. Within two years, I would have twelve members, plus administration staff. We used all of the space, and that year, we sold 198 homes.

There is great importance in surrounding yourself with the right people, not only in your personal life but professionally as well. I've been building my real estate team since 2006, and I've had 24 people come and go, which is normal.

As much as we'd love people to come and stay for the long term, it has to make sense with their goals. Sometimes their goals are to learn and then move on and build a team of their own. For others, the business wasn't right for them, so they decided to change industries altogether. Some move forward and become an independent agent after learning the ins and outs. There's always that kind of turnover on a team, but we also have people who have stayed long term.

The most extended team member with me is Mila Kolovic. She works with us in Kitchener, and she's now running the entire team! Mila is very, very loyal, she's had many other offers to leave and join other teams, but she decided to stay with me simply because she appreciates the way that I do business and the way that we work together. It's always a beautiful thing to have loyalty like that alongside you.

My son, Skyler, has been on our team for six years. He looks after all of the rentals and property management as well as selling homes. Skyler is twenty-seven years old and is as loyal as a son can be. I'm very proud of him.

The other team members we have right now are Ryan Moore, and he's already onto his third year with us and a great asset for the team. We are very fortunate to have Tammy Bannon, who is our coach. Tammy coaches the team on sales and personal growth because she's a Neuro-Linguistic Programming (NLP) coach. And we have Ash Zamani, Karen Fielding, James Paraschuk & Courtney Sprout, who have all recently joined the team.

Also, we have Benjamin May, who specializes in doing investment real estate. I met Ben seven years ago at TD CANADA Trust when I was depositing some of my commission cheques. We got to talking and I asked him if he had ever considered a career in real estate. It turned out he was in phase two of getting his licence. After that day, he came to our brokerage to meet with us. Within one year, he joined my team. Benjamin also has his license in Nova Scotia with a Keller Williams office there, which enables him to sell real estate in more than one province.

The CC Realty team is vastly growing. We have our Operations Manager, John Dewar. He has been with me since October of 2010 as well, so he's a very long-time and loyal employee. He makes all of our lives easier on the sales team as he looks after all of the administrative details that are so important in each deal. It does make it easier when you work well together for an extended period of time.

Michelle Carty would officially partner with me at Keller Williams in 2017. I have my team in Kitchener, and Michelle orchestrates the second team in Burlington, Ontario.

How did this partnership officially take shape? Let me take you through our journey.

As you know, Michelle and I met and worked together at CDI, and we were alongside one another again at Trios College, where we were reps in both Mississauga and Kitchener. After Trios, Michelle and I went our separate ways but remained in touch. Michelle didn't plan on getting into real estate, but she saw the way I turned my life around when I got into the business. It caught her interest, and it gave her the nudge to begin to consider getting into the industry. At the time, Michelle was pregnant with her third child. Thinking it would be the perfect time to study while on maternity leave from the job she had at the time, she went out and got ready to start taking her first course in real estate (the same one I did). Michelle bought a laptop, and everything else she would need to study, but in the midst of this, her pregnancy ended earlier than expected. Her baby was born at one pound, an actual miracle baby if you will. This wasn't the right time in her life to take a jump into a new arena, so she didn't open the books, but we continued to keep in touch. And when Michelle and her husband, Carl, went to buy their first investment property in 2014, it was me they called! Once Michelle got the property, I could see the wheels turning in her mind once again. She was now an investor and, she confessed to me; she was getting the real estate itch, big time! Carl even said, "Michelle, Roy, and I know you better than anyone. We know what you're capable of, get your licence!" The only problem was; Michelle was worried about the exams, but she was motivated and had that high energy, so she was able to buckle down and gave it her best shot. She took a deep breath and began to study. Instead of listening to music, she recorded every real estate course to ensure the information sunk in. I admired her for that!

While Michelle was working on getting her license, Keller Williams had come out with what they call an expansion system operation, which was a course teaching us how to have another team in another office (a market centre). I thought this would be the perfect way to partner with someone. And so I said to Michelle, "Do you want to do this? Do you want to build a team together, or do you want to be an agent on your own? And, by the way, you should join Keller Williams instead of any other brokerage because they have the best training."

Michelle turned around and said to me, "I want to understand your vision first!"

I replied by saying, "My vision is to grow the business, and have you help me do it because you have the energy to do it. You get things done, so I know you'll be a great partner if you want to do this with me."

So, she did her research, and ultimately, agreed, as she had no interest in becoming an independent REALTOR®. She observed what I brought to the table with sales and referrals, and she knew she could bring the missing piece to the table—the HR piece. Her brilliant idea was to replicate what I've been doing to set up agents for success. She said to me, "If you want to take things to the next level, we have to give people a reason to stay with us."

Michelle began to observe my team to see how they were working in the field. Her goal was to set up each person so that they were doing what they enjoyed while modelling the work I've been doing. We want agents to be able to love what they do and allow them to not worry about the admin work that they may not have to do. It's all about investing back into your business, that's the vision Michelle paints.

When Michelle got her license, she thanked me for giving her the push she needed. We began to build our CC team(s) in Burlington and Kitchener. Michelle loves being a part of Keller Williams because they are a training company. She also appreciated that KW is the only brokerage out there that understood the real estate culture, and how to measure it because that is the wheelhouse she came from. She knew Keller Williams was the right fit for her. Another recognition that Keller Williams has received is an acknowledgment by Career Bliss as being one of the "happiest companies to work for." And they began to position themselves as a technology company in 2017, which is where Michelle comes in again with her background. She knew that technology would play a significant role in the success of our team.

Be mindful of the environment that surrounds you because these are the people who are going to support your mission. I liked Michelle's energy, and I knew that we were going to be able to create magic together. At the end of the day, it's just business, but the right relationships are critical. I learned that we aren't all going to be good at everything. That's why it's essential to surround yourself with the right people, who make up for what you lack. Once you do that, you're on track to becoming successful in any type of business. Different input is excellent to bring together the big picture.

On Michelle's team, we now have Cindy Zupanovic, who came to us, left the team, and came back, which is very interesting because it says to us that she realized it's not necessarily better in any other place than with us. Cindy is now our Halton, Peel & Hamilton regional Partner. We also have Tanya Idzanovic and Nicole Ransome, who recently joined the team in Burlington, both great new additions. Michelle's daughter, Jovi Carty, works with us as well as an Internal Sales Agent and Michelle's Mom, Gloria Duguay is a great help with special events. And we also have Ryan Gumbert, who is our Marketing Manager now.

He started as an ISA (Internal Sales Agent), and he has incredible skills for websites, the internet and social media.

Keller Williams helps you look and think bigger, which has opened up my mind as a businessman. Today, Michelle and I have built a strong team that keeps growing. I have also partnered with Keller Williams Golden Triangle Realty. It's incredible to think that a group of people from different backgrounds can come together to create. There is a lot more success as a team rather than one individual working and building on their own.

Building lasting business relationships and partnerships is something that I strive to do, and I will go further into the connections I have formed along the way, later in my book. Until then, I hope you took notes on what it takes to build a successful team.

The CC Realty Group Kitchener- Waterloo Team.

Our Team Motto:
CC = Compassion and Commitment

Mission, Vision, Values:

Our **mission** is to exceed your Real Estate goals through superior communication and a team synergy of selling combined with compassion and commitment in all things.

Vision:

To be your complete Real Estate Team For Life!

Values we believe in:

- Family before business
- Customer enthusiasm
- No transaction is worth our reputation
- Who we are in business with really matters
- Personal growth through education
- Helping others achieve their goals
- Compassion and commitment in all things

Chapter Six

Family First

Behind every hard-working man is a family or group of people pushing him to reach his highest potential. Growing up, my family and friends had a major impact on the way I viewed the world in different ways.

When it comes to my parents, both of them had a positive influence on my life. They were both affectionate and showed me the kind of love every young man needs. My dad, Mel, passed away in 2005 from cancer. I miss him often and hold onto the wisdom he has shared with me over the years. My dad taught me how to be handy by getting me involved with things around the house when I was a young man. I appreciate my dad for who he was as a person and how he raised me. Although he did teach me how to be somewhat handy around the house, I can genuinely say that I was never half as handy as he was.

When my dad was in his 50s, he was laid off from his job at Harlock Schultz Electric. He was the bookkeeper there, but they were being bought out by a more prominent electrical company, and because that function was centralized, he was made redundant.

I was annoyed that he was laid-off from the company he had dedicated over twenty years of his life to, but my dad was quick to change my perspective on it all. As I felt it was a shame he was being put out, my dad turned to me and said, "You know what Roy, they are more than fair to me. They are giving me a year's notice. This is just the change that comes with the territory, and worrying about it does not help, so I'm not going to worry! I'll go on to find another job, whatever that may be." Because of conversations like that with my father, I have learned not to worry. I always look forward, positively!

The attitude that I observed within my father have helped me to understand things on a deeper level. I was able to relax as I watched things work out for him. He was thrilled to retire early and spend even more time with my mom, which is a beautiful thing.

Since my dad has passed, my mom, Penny, has moved closer to my home and my sister's home here in Kitchener so that we can see each other more often. She has always been the ultimate guiding force in my life. I'm very close with her, visiting her each week, as much as I possibly can. My sister, Diane, is eighteen months older than me. Growing up, we fought like cats and dogs, as many siblings do. Once she moved out of the house, that changed. Today, we are so much closer than we ever were when we were kids.

You've heard me talk about Nikki and our adventures along the way. Well, today, we have been married for thirty-three years. Nikki and I also come from parents who have devoted their lives to their spouses and have never broken up. Our parents have over the fifty-years under their belt, and Nikki and I are in our 33rd year of marriage. I'm beyond grateful for Nikki. She has stuck with me through the good times and the not so good times, as we learned some things in business and in life along the way. We have two boys together; Skyler is twenty-seven, and Jagger is twenty-five. Skyler works with me in the business, taking care of all the rental and property management and Jagger, what can I say, he sure lives up to his name. He loves music and is in a band called 'Rocket Bomb.' I know he'll be an overnight success! (as many musicians are—after many nights). You can already find their hits on Apple Music and Spotify for download.

Family is my number one priority, that's why I have always liked to work with family members and partner with friends while I travel. I have travelled all across Europe: Spain, France, England, and Italy. I've also been to Greece and Turkey, but for the most part, Nikki and I love cruises. Travelling and movies have always been my main hobbies outside of work. I'm not particularly eager to spend money on material things, never have. Real estate and travel are how I choose to spend my money. Buying real estate is to create generational wealth and travelling around the world is the way I reward myself.

If I had to live in one place, though, it would be Maui, Hawaii—great weather, an easygoing lifestyle, yet all the comforts of home.

My family and I continue to travel around the world. And we enjoy spending time together while we take on new adventures.

My 'Family First' mindset is shown in all that we do. With our clients, we tell them that their family is more important to us than any real estate transaction. And that means that if they have a family member that is not feeling well, then let us know and we can modify any showings planned for the house so that it can be when the family is well again.

For our teammates, as soon as they need time for their family, we arrange coverage so that they can go and be with their family as needed. 'Family First,' Business Second.

Nikki and me on vacation together in Greece.

On vacation with Nikki and Pauline Delaney and Scott Harris in Hawaii celebrating another real estate investment together.

Chapter Seven

Mindset

A strong mindset is the ticket holder to becoming a successful person, not only in the real estate world but in all aspects of life. Once you have the right mindset, things will start happening for you, not to you. Believe you can achieve your goals first, and the rest follows. That's the law of attraction.

Years ago, I had my second near-death experience. I was out for a leisurely ride on my motorcycle when every motorcyclist's nightmare happened. As I watched another vehicle head straight for me, it was as if it was happening in slow motion. I thought maybe if I try to get in front of the car, perhaps I can avoid the collision, but as I tried, he still pulled across my lane in front of me. I hit the side of his car, which threw me into a Kentucky Fried Chicken parking lot. I knew this one was going to hurt. Thank God I had my protective gear on; all I could think while I was laying there, wow, am I ever lucky! If I landed wrong or if I didn't have gear, it could have been game over for me.

When I was lying in a hospital bed, I reflected on the fact that we really can't control everything that happens to us. I tried to avoid that accident; I turned in towards the curb. And I was dreaming in my mind in those few seconds that the other vehicle was going to stop.

I genuinely believe that he didn't see me whatsoever, so he kept going. Because I angled a little bit to the right, thinking I could get in front of him, it made me land in the parking lot, instead of landing on the road, or the curb of the roadway. I realized that was no coincidence. Everything happens for a reason.

I said to my mom, "Are you going to call the lawyer, or am I?" I felt I should have something for the suffering I had endured. And I knew, as much as the gentleman didn't see me, he has insurance for those things, and so do we, so that's why I made the decision to call a lawyer. It's those kinds of little choices that you make in a moment of contemplation that could change your life dramatically. If I hadn't got a lawyer, if we hadn't got a settlement, it very well might have been years and years before I would buy a home, and I wouldn't have the same sort of equity that I was able to gain by buying a house sooner. See, things do happen for a reason. At that time, my mindset developed. I realized the good that came out of it. I realized that things happen for you, not to you.

I think any time you have a near-death experience like that, it puts you in a much better frame of mind for the rest of your life. Before the accident, I thought I was a fairly positive person. However, one can't help but second guess things. Am I going to be able to walk again? Am I going to be able to do the things I was doing before? Am I going to be a whole man still? The answer is yes! All I had to do was change the way I looked at it. Some may find this difficult to do because of maybe, the way they were brought up or the way they were taught from other people. We often respond unfavourably, especially if there's some hurt, and that's normal. I like to call that your first gut thought. And then, once you give it a second thought, sometimes, you realize it's not so bad. You can work it out another way.

Despite the fact that it was a negative thing that happened, I started to see the good in it. In the future, I would look at the positive in everything, no matter how negative it may seem at the time. There's so much good in life, and if you look on the positive side, you're going to find it! I continue to remain a positive man throughout the good and bad times. Not only that, but I always search out to find the good that other people are doing and then I ask to work with them.

Mindset is a choice. It is an established set of attitudes held by someone. You can choose to be happy, or you can choose to be negative. If you drop the soap in the shower, does that ruin your day or do you say that 99% of the day has gone right so far?

Another example I can share with you about changing the way you look at things is when I was in New Orleans. I was at a company convention where we were treated to an evening out on a classic steam paddleboat. Before I parked my rental van, I called the parking lot company, and I said:

"I'm kind of unclear how long this boat cruise goes, how much do I need to put in?"

I bought a ticket for, let's say, four hours, and in the end, it was five hours. As we came back off the boat, walking towards the van, I noticed there's one of those clamps on the tire with a big sticker on the window. I shook my head and chuckled because I knew the value of the dollar on those puppies were high. Right away, we were thinking, how do we get back to our hotel room?

Your initial reaction is; "Oh, this is gonna be painful, this is going to cost some serious coin, we might have to wait a while, and how are we gonna get back to our hotel room?"

And then I changed my mind on it, and I simply said, "First, I take responsibility, it's my fault. I should have put in an extra hour, just in case." It's really not up to them. They don't know how long the boat is going to take.

I held myself accountable for it, and once I did that, I didn't feel angry anymore. And, yes, it's going to cost some money. However, with Keller Williams, I thought, "I have a profit-sharing, instead of the money that is due to me, I can use a portion of the extra money to help pay for nasty little surprises like this." Suddenly my whole feeling about the situation is one of, "It's all right, it's all right, it doesn't really matter. In fact, let's make fun of it."

We called the number on the window, and the guy was still in the parking lot, and he actually came over and took the boot off right away. We paid him what we owed immediately. Because of that, there was a discount. It would cost more if they hadn't come back, and we would have had to wait longer. See, it all worked out.

I said to the guy, "Please, let me take a selfie with you because I'm gonna post this on Facebook to show what a good time we're having down here despite this parking ticket thing." I know that I made his day as he told me that he usually gets yelled at instead of embraced with fun.

After that, to help other people, I decided to give the people going out after us a heads-up. "Hey, if you're going out on this boat, by the way, you need five hours parking, not four."

We all laughed. I had a whole bunch of people with me in the van, and they all laughed, and we just made so much fun of it that it's just an experience to tell people, instead of one of pain. Instead of saying, "New Orleans sucks, I got a ticket," I changed my perspective.

It all comes down to mindset. When you have a great mindset, and you put your mind in the right place, then these kinds of negative things just don't hurt you the way they would if you dwell on them.

You have to know that things are going to work out. Like my dad always taught me growing up, he always knew that things were going to work out for the best. He would tell me not to worry about anything. His way of thinking paved the way to many extraordinary opportunities in my life, and I thank my dad for passing that onto me.

Each day, I continue to look for the positives in every situation and in each person that I meet. I choose to be grateful and take responsibility for all things in my life—especially my decisions. I learn from the bad, but I don't stay stuck in it. That's the key to staying confident in myself. Not only do I recommend being happy with yourself as a person but choose to be happy for others and their accomplishments, too!

Chapter Eight

Inspiration

With a healthy mindset, comes the quest for inspiration. In real estate, it's essential to surround yourself with people who will encourage you to take you and your business to the next level.

I've explained how I've always been a positive person in the previous chapters. Instead of taking away from a person, I like to add happiness and value to their life. An extrovert to the core, if I'm left alone too long, you better believe I'll be seeking people out, whether it's by phone or in person or on the internet. I like the company of people.

I'm an early bird too. In the morning, I wake up between six or seven am, as I take my first morning breaths with gratitude for being alive and all that I am and all that I have. Then, I'll turn on one of my favourite shows, have breakfast, and I'm out the door.

I'm a big fan of audible.com. On the way to the office, I listen to audiobooks like Darren Hardy——also known as Darren Daily (Monday to Friday for Words of Wisdom), Tony Robbins, and Grant Cardone. I walk into work, pumped up and full of inspiration, just after 9 a.m.

If you ever want to listen to short stories of underdogs fighting against all the odds to get out of their mundane lives, facing all their fears and all obstacles, then tune into Darren Daily, which is one of the best! He interviews many great people with mind-blowing inspirational insights.

Like Darren Hardy, both of my grandfathers had a significant effect on me growing up. Both were entrepreneurs, and that was fascinating to me. They each had their own business and the freedom that comes with being your own boss, which appealed to me. I wanted to be just like them. They got up each day and made things happen.

My Grandfather on my mom's side, Ralph, was a successful accountant. Ralph came to Canada from England and started with no clients at all. He continually reached out to people to become their accountant until he had a thriving business that he enjoyed doing right into his retirement years.

My Grandfather on my dad's side, Elmer, worked for the Toronto Transit Commission (TTC) and realized that he wanted the freedom of his own business. He soon purchased a gas station and cottage rental units near Orillia, Ontario, moving away from the big city. Eventually, Elmer would move to Guelph to live and own a gas station in Rockwood (nearby Guelph), and it was at the church in Guelph where my Mother and Father met and got married.

Seeing both of my Grandparents benefiting from being entrepreneurs and probably having the same genes from these two certainly made an inner drive in me to be an entrepreneur.

One of my favourite daily affirmations that I would say to myself is: "I'm an opportunity magnet. Many wonderful things will happen for me today. Money flows freely in my direction. My body and soul are healthy and strong!" My entire team recites this out loud with me each morning Monday to Friday in the office as we prepare ourselves for our next two hours of lead generation. Lead generation means reaching out to people to see who we can next help buy, sell, or invest in real estate.

You heard me mention my friend and Mortgage Broker, Roy Singh who had his own office, Roy once said to me, "You may as well get your mortgage license." It's this unsolicited guidance that helped me become more knowledgeable and have other streams of income. I listened to Roy because I respected what he had to say and what he brought to the table.

Inspiration comes in many forms and from many different people who come into your life. Whether it's for a season or a lifetime, I appreciate each person who has inspired me to better myself.

The people I met along the way have inspired me to want to give back as much as humanly possible. I believe giving is our duty, no matter what our financial status is. We all have the capabilities to impact others' lives by lending a helping hand and giving back somehow.

Giving First:

I joined the Optimist Club in 2003 before I became a REALTOR® because I was looking for a way to connect with the community and contribute in some way. The optimist club is one of the most affordable service clubs. Many of the other clubs out there charged member fees as high as $500 per year or more. I wasn't prepared to pay that back then, as I did not have a large income at the time. I was the only one working in my family at that point in my life.

I knew I wanted to join the Optimist Club for many reasons, the optimist creed being one of them. It resonated with who I am as a person and how I view the world.

Here is the Optimist Creed:

PROMISE YOURSELF -

To be so strong that nothing can disturb your peace of mind.

To talk health, happiness, and prosperity to every person you meet.

To make your friends feel that there is something in them.

To look at the sunny side of everything and make your optimism come true.

To think only of the best, to work only for the best and to expect only the best.

To be just as enthusiastic about the success of others as you are about your own.

To forget the mistakes of the past and press on to the greater achievements of the future.

*To wear a cheerful countenance at all times and
give every living creature you meet a smile.*

*To give so much time to the improvement of yourself that you have
no time to criticize others*

*To be too large for worry, too noble for anger, too strong for fear, and too happy to
permit the presence of trouble.*

-OPTIMIST INTERNATIONAL

The Optimist Creed is the way that I feel; about life and how I view the people I interact with because I always look at the bright side of everything, and I search for the positive aspects of everyone I meet as I navigate my way through my journey. For me, this was a match. The interesting thing is; once I became a member at the Optimist Club and began to go to meetings, the other members started to ask me a lot of questions about real estate. Before too long, Dean (one of the members), asked me to help him and his wife purchase a home they saw at an open house. This was the first of many deals I would do with the Optimist Club, and it was effortless. I offered to be of service, and they were happy to have me help them. We are all like-minded that way. And the connections went beyond the members; their children also reached out for help. It was interesting that Rick and his wife, Aldene, introduced me to their daughter, Sheryl, who had just landed a teaching job and was looking to purchase a new home! Not only did I help Sheryl, but I also ended up helping her five bridesmaids. It was quite incredible when her mom pulled out the picture to show me her wedding pictures (Sheryl had got married right after I helped her buy her home), and I realized that I had helped each and every one of her bride's maids buy a home. It's moments like this when you get to see what hard work and meaningful work can create.

What I learned along the way is that it's best to give first. I simply wanted to give to the Optimist Club, and the Optimist Club ended up giving back to me in a really big way. I'm truly grateful that I became a member of the Optimist Club, and I'm still a member there, to this day.

Chapter Nine

Dancing With Lady Luck

I'm sure that everybody has had at least one dance with Lady Luck in their lives. I, on the other hand, have always been a very lucky guy, and that doesn't hurt in the least when you're trying to make a million dollars. Some would call it 'luck,' some may say, 'by accident.'

I started buying some of the Canadian Cancer Society lottery tickets years ago after my father had passed from cancer in 2005. I remember I would purchase them over the phone, or I'd order them online. At the time, I had been buying them quite often, and I started to win with the tickets ($1000 here and there) when all of a sudden, I hit the mother-load! I had won a suitcase, as some would say, ha-ha!

For one of the draws, I had bought three tickets, and I had forgotten that I made that purchase. The lottery agents called me one day asking if I had any. I said, "No, I don't think I bought any yet." Well, I had already bought some, now I accidentally bought three more. The draw was on April 1st, so I now have six lottery tickets from the same lottery when a call came in on April 1, 2011, saying, "Congratulations!" They called the house first, and Nikki answered, thinking that they were looking for a donation or something. She told them that I was going to be home later, thinking she was going to play a joke on me and hung up on them, the same way some of us hang up on telemarketers.

Afterward, a friend of mine had sent me an email (another REALTOR®), and he says, "Congratulations, you're very deserving, and God bless you!" He continued to write, "Congratulations on winning the lottery!" I was confused, and then it hit me. It's April fools! No one's going to trick me this year, I thought. I ended up playing dumb and asked him back, "Is this an April fool's joke or something?" The more I thought about it, he was a pretty religious older gentleman, and I didn't believe that he would joke about something like this.

When I got home later that day, I had asked Nikki if the Canadian Cancer Society had called. She said, "yeah, they did, but I told them that you would be home later and to call back." Luckily, she got their number, so I called them back. Sure enough, I did win! They said, "Yes, you won a Car! You won a 2011 Infiniti G37." I was ecstatic. Both my wife and I were jumping around arm and arm around the kitchen. Then we could hear a faint voice over the phone, "excuse me, excuse me, so are going to take the car?" That was a great question.

We didn't need another car. I was already driving a Lexus, and the G37 was a sports car that was RWD. With our Canadian winters, that may not be a good idea to have so, I had asked them what the cash value was, and they said, "$38,000." I asked them, "how many people take cash instead of the car?" They said, "99.5%. Almost everyone takes cash." I wanted to make sure, so I waited for a week, and we went to test-drove the Infiniti G37 at the local dealer.

After the test drive, my son, Skyler, said: "Dad, I love Infiniti's! You should get the car."

He continued,

"That way, I can drive it!"

I chuckled and said, "Son, you should not be driving any car worth more than $5,000."

And sure enough, within that same year, he ended up totalling his car. Thank God, Skyler bounces well. He has now totalled two cars, and both times came out without a scratch!

We really did give the car a chance, but ultimately the money was a better choice. So, I picked up the phone and said, "well, send me the money!" and, of course, with that money, I bought another property (in Florida), which I knew was a much better investment. I was so lucky to win the lottery, lucky the car was RWD, and smart that I said, "No, send me the money." And happy that they did.

After that, I continued to buy lottery tickets—one in the fall and one in the spring. The fall ticket was called the Cancer Society Daffodil Daily Lottery. Well, in September of that same year, they had called me again, and the funny thing was that it was the same lady, Janice Gray. She works for the Ontario Lottery Corporation (O.L.G.). That must be the best job out there, right (calling people to let them know that they just won the lottery)?

This time when Janice called, she told me that I had won the daily lottery of $5,000. Her first question over the phone was, "Would you like us to send the cheque to the same address in Kitchener?" I exclaimed, "Of course, Janice, that would be great!" All the while, laughing and shaking my head. My whole team laughed as well, "Boy, oh boy, you are one lucky S.O.B."

A few days had passed, and Janice Gray stayed faithful to her word. The cheque arrived for $5k, and guess what I did? Yup, you guessed it. I bought another property, and this was one of those properties where a client had said to me: "Hey, you should buy the one next door?"

These clients were so awesome. I took them to The East Forest Sales Centre. I think they had like six homes left. Because my clients were Chinese, they didn't like the one with the address 214. In their culture, it was very unlucky to have the number four in the address, so they bought 216 instead. That's when they said, "Roy, why don't you buy the one next door and be our neighbour" (even though we weren't going to live there). It was just like the situation with another client, where we bought on the same street. I said, "Yeah, why don't I?" They drew up a contract for them and me, a double whammy!

The fantastic thing, back then, you could buy a rental at 5% down, and the Builder could give you a rebate. The Builder was offering a rebate of $7,500. Then they would let us apply our commission to the down payment. I did it and put the commission towards the down payment, using the $7,500 from the Builder. That covered the 5% down payment requirement, so then all I had to pay for were the lawyer fees, land transfer tax, and other closing costs, which I took out of the commission from one that I had sold to my clients.

Now I have this beautiful brand-new townhouse with three bedrooms and three bathrooms, a single car garage for zero dollars, and it's completely free. Talk about horseshoes, and it gets even better. I rented the property out for $1,250 per month, and with a mortgage of $1,200, that meant I was putting back into my pocket $50 per month. That was in the beginning stages, since then the prices for rent have gone up, and now I have it rented out for $2,000/mth, which is phenomenal. It's the gift that keeps giving and giving, like winning the cash for life lottery.

Another aspect of my real estate investing strategy is rent-to-own properties. Here is an experience that turned out to be one of the best ideas I have ever learned about and had the pleasure of implementing in my strategy for investment.

The property I was approached about was on the west side of Kitchener. A gentleman who was a rent-to-own tenant was looking to find a buyer to replace his current owner. He called and asked if I would consider taking over another person's rent-to-own property?

Without any hesitation, I said, of course, we would consider it. The owner lived out of town, and he wanted to get his money out. That was in 2016. By now, the prices were creeping up, and the owner realized that he could make some money on his investment. The tenant wasn't really in any position to continue paying for it as a rent-to-own. He offered it to me at a reasonable price if I would look after money owed to the tenant from the rent-to-own deal he had done. So, in short, the way we had to structure this deal was we would payout $15,000 to the tenant because he owed the tenant this money that he saved up in the rent-to-own program.

It was rather tricky to get a mortgage at that time. I knew I would have to bring a business partner in on the deal to help save the tenant and help the owner get out. So, here's what happened. We said to the tenant that we were going to buy the property and we would become his new landlord. The $15,000 that was owed to the tenant, we took care of by not charging him rent for the next seven months. I think it was roughly $2,200/ month, which covered all of the expenses. His eyes lit up when we told him the plan! I knew he was in for sure.

At the time, we had paid $360,000 for the property, minus the $15,000, so we got it for $345,000, but we had to carry no payments for nine months, which was doable for my investment partner and me. We knew the property was going up in value, so we bought it using our line of credit. Within six months of purchase, we had it reappraised, and it came in at $420,000. Then we got a mortgage that gave us all our money back except $12,000. Now we own the property for $12,000, and yes, we had some carrying costs, so it wasn't completely free. However, this is where the story gets really good…

The following year, 2017, the market prices skyrocketed, at which point we had it reappraised, and now it came in at $600,000. Yeah, baby, it was like we were walking along and tripping over a suitcase full of money. Now, we were able to pull out $150,000 tax-free. The property didn't owe us anything, and we made a killing on it, this was better than getting just a free property it was as though someone paid us to take it and paid us handsomely. And this is the story of our house on the west side of Kitchener. To this day, we still have it rented and will continue to keep it rented out. This one was our little cash cow, and it will continue to get paid down with tenants that enjoy living there.

That was just an example of accidental luck due to a massive fluctuation in the marketplace. The market jumped 40% that year and that is not sustainable, it was entirely out of anyone's control. However, we can do a forced appreciation by doing renovations to properties or creating second suites.

What I would like to do in the near future is, find properties in which we can turn into duplexes. Ideally, a bungalow and renovate the basement into a legal conforming apartment and rent them out. Once they become two separate units now, we have it reappraised and pull our money out and let it pay itself down in rent and give us positive cash flow. So, in a way, a free property after it paid us out and a little cash box giving you money every month. We sure danced with Lady Luck throughout these ventures.

And these are the kind of ventures I would like to focus on converting moving forward!

Chapter Ten

Good Versus Great

Someone had asked me once: What is the difference between a good agent versus a great agent? Allow me to tell you about what I feel makes a great agent.

First, there's the service.

Service and being a speedy service is the number one thing that would set you apart from the rest.

When I first became a REALTOR® in 2003, real estate could take about a month to sell if you were good, and you took that time to find a house or two for your customers. Still, I wanted to be great! I began to work much faster than most, lightning-fast, to find customers. Not only to buy but also to sell. I would search every day for both; hence, I was committed. I held myself accountable to have a much higher level of commitment and to do my job to the best of my capability. I recruited my wife, Nikki, to help me with that. She would run the searches for houses every day to match my buyers and then she would send it to them with a personal note saying, "this one looks pretty good, let's go see it." That personal touch, along with how quickly I was able to find a house for each client to view, was what led me to a lot of buyer side deals.

Once a client would get to know me, they got to like me, then they would trust me and in turn, would work with me. By this time, they would buy with me and then sell with me, which would lead to more listings, which equaled more money for my family and me. **Always under-promise and over-deliver.**

My friend had asked me one day, "How long is it before you make a million?"

Well, the year that he had asked me that question, I was well underway to selling 98 homes, and that was just with my wife and myself. I knew I needed help to keep achieving my goals. That is when I started to build my team, in my third year as a REALTOR®. I thought to myself, Oh buddy, I'm just getting warmed up! I chuckled.

I never forgot when my brother-in-law, Chris Abbott, invited me to the Whitney Canada course all those years ago. I also remembered what he said to me when I asked, "why me?" He had a brother. Why didn't he ask him? I thought. He told me back then, "Roy, you are the one person that I knew would say yes, knowing fully that everyone else would have said no." I believe it was because of my personality that he chose me. Who I am set the stage for what I'm meant to be doing, and the people who helped me get to each stage in my career are a true example of the synchronicities that shaped me. **When people present you with opportunities, take them. Say, yes, more often than, no!**

Not all of my real estate investments were planned ones, aside from the first one that didn't work out so well. Some of the other ones that came along from being a REALTOR®, a lot of them I invested in actually by accident simply because of my clients. Many times, in helping tenants with Rent–to–own, I would be the investor holding the property.

Sometimes things happen, maybe through timing or by accident. It's those little choices and actions that led me to become a millionaire and then a multi-millionaire. My real estate holdings are well into the millions now. I was buying a lot of properties, although many were a thought-through purchase, a few were accidental because of my clients saying you should buy that property. I find it amazing how some people do influence you, and you do something without even thinking it through.

Part One: Property Management

In 2010, two of my good friends and clients of mine, Toby and Janina Struewing, purchased two townhouses and two condos. They were using them as rental investment properties. Within a year, they had decided that they didn't like the property management company that was looking after the filling up of the properties and turning over the tenants. So, one day, Toby calls me up and says, "Roy, you would do a better job at property-managing these places. I will pay you the same as the property management company I was using if you would so kindly do property management for us?" I said: "Yes, of course!" And just like that, by accident, I'm now in the property management business. When opportunities come knocking, open the door!

As I help more and more people buy investment properties, I realized that I might as well offer to look after their homes under property management at the same time. This became a new revenue source for me, and it has grown so big that we now manage over 70 homes. The expansion has allowed me to pass the job on to my son, Skyler Cleeves. It has become Skyler's main focus, and we have just hired an assistant to help him because as the number of properties grows, so does the number of tenants and the number of calls.

Me with My Son, Skyler Cleeves, & our Mini

Getting into the property management business was never the plan. It happened by accident, through seizing opportunities that were presented to me at any given time. This really happened by accident, and now it's helped lead me to the millionaire lifestyle.

Part Two: Thinking Outside the Box (The Art of a Deal)

In the summer of 2014, a builder that I had met (a forward-thinking man) asked me if I would like to buy a house that he had built in Listowel. It was a beautiful bungalow with three bedrooms up, and he also offered to finish the basement and make a second entrance down there. The price they wanted to sell it at was $250,000, and I felt this was a very fair price for purchase. I worked to get a mortgage, and I found that the lenders were holding back financing to my company due to the large number of homes that I already had a mortgage on (even though they were cash-flow positive and my income and credit were strong). They still didn't want to take the risk, more mortgages that were for rental purposes specifically.

Rather than throw in the towel and tell the owner I couldn't get the mortgage, I thought about how I could think outside the box and still make the deal with him, one that would be beneficial to both him and me.

As I went to bed that night, I was rolling around, thinking through things in my mind, and eventually came up with a proposal. I made it as simple as one page.

Here is an outline of the agreement as an example:

July 31, 2014 Situation Recap

- Lenders are holding back financing to my company due to a large number of homes the company already holds—even though all are cash flow positive and have equity positions. Approval may come yet may take longer than desired and may even be a turndown or require undesirable rates, thereby negating the deal.
- You as sellers do not want to continue to pay interest for a home that they are not using.
- Mortgages are paid in arrears, so the 1st of August payment is for the month of July already gone by.
- Roy does want this property and has cash available to work with.

Agreement Points

- Roy pays the September 1st mortgage payments and onward until the home is Sold (to either Roy or another Buyer)
- Roy to reimburse the utilities and taxes on the home calculated from August 1st.

- Roy pays out $13,000 to you, the seller, to finish the basement—can start now or soon as it fits your schedule.

- Roy lists the home for sale and for Rent in the Seller's name—Seller to show the home while at the same time working on finishing the basement.

- Roy also loans to the Seller $10,000 - the amount that would be proceeds from the sale - so that Sellers can put that money to good use now. This loan is at zero Interest per year with NO payment until the home is sold and then paid back to Roy from the proceeds of the sale.

- Out of the Sale, Sellers to Net $250,000 after all commission for real estate, paid less than half of the legal fees. Any balance above that amount is to be paid to Roy.

Agreed: July 31st, 2014, with signatures from all parties, including myself.

All done in simple bullet form, just to cover the points of our agreement. We both signed this in July 2014. I managed that property and eventually sold it two years later, in 2016, at a profit for both of us.

This deal allowed me to think outside the box when it comes to investing in real estate. It makes sense to have partners, and in this case, the seller was basically my partner to help me do the same as purchase this home and ultimately sell it for a profit. And this met all of the seller's goals as well.

It pays to think outside the box and partner with the right people. You'd be surprised at how ready and able many of your partners will be to work with you on the basis that is different from what everyone else was thinking. Don't be scared to ask.

And again, this came mostly because it was offered to me to purchase, rather than targeting it as a purchase. How lucky am I?

Part Three: Great Partnerships

If you've been presented with an opportunity, I believe, it's always in your best interest to take it. It's great to be open to new partnerships. Building with others benefits everyone involved if your skills complement one another. That is what has happened with many of the partnerships I've created. Having people around you, on the same mission as you, is what it's all about. Together, you're more powerful. Yes, you can make things happen on your own, but you can make things happen in a bigger way and better way with others by your side. Investing with others has created a comfortable flow in my life. Not only that, but it has also allowed me to have more leisure too. I'm able to do what I want to do with the people I love. I'm grateful to all of the individuals I have partnered with, in my life: my wife, Nikki, my business partnerships, and the investments I have made that have brought me to become a millionaire. By accident, yes, but with the help of others, it has kept the momentum going.

Along with partnering with Michelle Carty and the other relationships I have shared with you in my story, I have formed several other successful ties along the way that have made all the difference in helping me make smart investments.

Working with Quality Partners will increase your luck and theirs too!

I have a very good high school friend named Scott Harris. Scott and I were locker mates and had classes together in school. We enjoyed our time together and our love of music, but we lost touch with each other during our university years. Scott went to Western University in London, Ontario, and as you know, I went to Wilfrid Laurier University in Waterloo, Ontario.

Years later, we reconnected when we were both out in the working world, and it was because both of our moms were doing genealogy together and said, "Let's help the boys reconnect." We asked for each other's phone numbers as Facebook was not as prevalent at this time. I discovered Scott lived very close to a campus that I was planning to attend on the far side of Toronto. I realized it would be so much easier for me to stay at his place for a few days rather than drive back-and-forth from where I was living.

I called Scott and said, "Hey buddy, would it be okay if I came and stayed a few nights?"

And he said, "let me check," as he had just started to live with a wonderful gal named Pauline Delaney.

Now Pauline is that independent type of girl that said, "Hey, if your friend wants to come in, and it's okay with you, by all means, let them come and stay in the spare room."

Pauline and I became good friends as well and in time when she met my wife Nikki, they too, became the best of friends. It was not too long before all four of us were doing family vacations together, including cruises and resorts days, etc.

Because I love real estate and enjoy investing in it, I could not help but talk about it all the time, and this included while I was on vacation. I would ask Scott and Pauline if they would consider investing in real estate and I would talk about the deals that I had done and how they had made me money.

Scott was always interested, and Pauline was always cautious, and this is often the way, and it's a good balance. And Scott, being a good husband, said, "No, we will probably just purchase something for Pauline's brother if anything to help him out." Soon after that, Scott and Pauline had their home appraised and found it was worth $800,000 with only $32,000 owing on it! This made them realize that there is a lot of dead equity sitting there, and we could use that money to make money much the way the right has been talking about. Since this time, Scott and Pauline, have bought over a dozen homes. They have many rentals now and have done many rent-to-owns in conjunction with Nikki and me.

Scott and Pauline have been a great help to Nikki and me. I was at a point where I could not get additional mortgages on my own, and Scott and Pauline had the capacity to continue to finance, which made all the difference for us to be able to continue to grow. Together, we have made hundreds of thousands of dollars collectively. To this day, we continue to travel together. We even enjoy upgrades on our travels now as the result of finding one another and working together on these real estate investments.

I cannot help but think how differently things might have turned out if Pauline said, "I don't know your friend Roy and maybe he should just get a hotel and just come and see us one night instead of staying over." For sure, we would not have made the same bond, and for sure, we may not have ended up on all of these beautiful vacations together, and all of the investing that brought us together.

Who is Thomas Wong? Let me tell you about this incredible man.

Thomas Wong is an entrepreneur and seasoned investor in real estate. He's a great mentor and a pleasure to have as another one of my business partners in investing.

You see, Thomas Wong is the man who trained me on rent-to-owns. His parents lived beside my business partner David Anderson. Thomas met Dave and decided to hire us to sell that house. Dave and I even helped paint some of the house to make it more saleable. Thomas noticed these actions and appreciated that we went the extra mile to help. Because of that, he decided he would share with us about his investments in rent-to-owns.

Thomas said to me, "I have an opportunity right now where you could be the owner of a property, and you only need to put in no four thousand dollars." Well, it turned out, I had the money readily available, and I decided right then and there that I would invest with Thomas. This was the start of a beautiful business relationship and a beautiful friendship as well.

Thomas and I have now done over forty rent-to-owns. We had experienced everything, from super-smooth sailing situations, where tenants end up buying the home early (before the traditional three-year timeframe) to scenarios where the rent-to-own- tenant either passed away or split up with their spouses and had to exit the program. When things like that would happen, we would calculate a new plan for that home.

As I write this book, Thomas and his brother, myself and my son have all decided to work together on future rent-to-owns, fixing flips, and even possibly BRRRR (Buy, Renovate, Rent, Reappraise, Repeat) properties.

When the "Why?" is big enough, you'll figure out the "How?," and this was the case in 2016 when I purchased three brand new properties. I knew that they wouldn't be built until 2018, and I could see that the prices were rising. The prices of the properties were based on prices off early 2016, not on what the price increases were going to be. So, knowing that all of the homes would most likely be worth about one-hundred thousand more in 2018, I decided to buy all three and figure out a way to finance them later.

By the time the houses were ready for me to take ownership, I had trouble getting mortgages since I already have over twelve mortgages. Once you have ten residential mortgages, the banks just don't want to give you another rental mortgage, even if you earn a lot of money and have exceptional credit. It was a challenge to formulate a plan to seal the deal on these three homes.

I talked to many of my investors about my dilemma, never asking for help and when I talked to Thomas, he immediately offered to lend a hand. Thomas said to me: "If you need some money to get you through until you have the financing, just let me know."

Thomas was true to his word and loaned me sufficient funds so I could close on all three properties. And with the help of Jeff Reitzel at Mortgage Alliance Canada's Mortgage choice, I was able to get mortgages on two out of three of the homes. This allowed me to pay back the money I borrowed from Thomas, with interest.

With the help of these two men, I was able to reach my goals. All I had to do was simply tell what my goals were and the challenges that I was having and they both came to help me achieve funding for additional properties and get them into my stable.

Even now, I have just purchased a triplex and a duplex, all sitting on one piece of land in Ingersoll, Ontario, with zero money down and everything financed.

How could I do this?

It was an exclusive listing that was referred to me by my mortgage broker, Gary Brown, from Mortgage Architects, and I had an opportunity for a vendor take-back where the seller will hold a 20% down payment if needed. Well, the seller is a lovely lady. She was heading back to Newfoundland, and I asked if she would accept at 3% interest only for three years as a vendor take back. She said, "Yes!"

Gary worked on getting me a mortgage and he did this by introducing me to the commercial division of a major bank to help me get this funded as a commercial property since, in total, there are five units instead of just three. The great news is, the bank is willing to fund this under their commercial umbrella. They will also provide me with a mortgage on that one property remaining that I did not get a mortgage on from 2018. This release of funds will allow me to go ahead and purchase more real estate. Onward, I climb, with a little help from my friends!

> **Tell people your goals and you will be surprised at how they will help you achieve them.**
> **- Roy Cleeves**

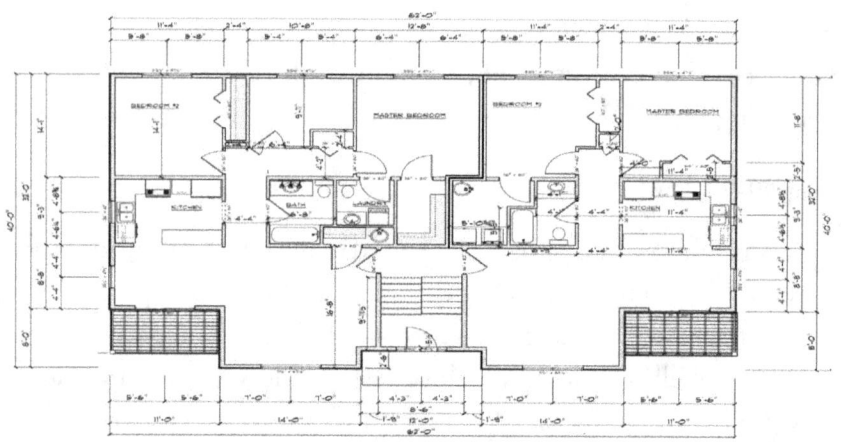

-One of our upcoming projects-

Chapter Eleven

Don't Be Afraid to Just Ask

In 2013, I met Benjamin May at the TD CANADA Trust bank while I was depositing some of my commission cheques. I thanked Ben for his assistance and told him that I would be happy to return the excellent service in real estate if he ever needed my help and also that if he ever wanted to be a REALTOR® to let me know as our office has the best training and would be his best nest for success.

As it turns out, Ben had already started to take his real estate license and was very interested in becoming a REALTOR®. Also, his eyes lit up when he saw the cheques that I deposited in my bank account. Ben would eventually decide to join us as soon as he got his license. In the meantime, he had a home that he needed to sell, which I helped him with and earned another commission. It really pays to ask people if you can help them when you are in the service industry.

Ben did very well for business yet always dreamed of owning an island and doing development for real estate. He then began to spend some time in Nova Scotia and even got his real estate license suitable for the Nova Scotia region.

During this time, Ben met a builder named Jeff, who was willing to work on a partnership basis to develop for a four-acre site in Liverpool, Nova Scotia. Upon hearing about his development, I was so excited for him that I let him know the next time that he was going to go to Nova Scotia, that I would be happy to go with him to see his development. I found this absolutely amazing, and I wanted to understand the opportunities that are out there because the numbers work better for investment with the prices being lower than in Ontario and the rent still being relatively high.

Ben and I made the trip, and during that time, I also met another Builder named Gerard that Ben was introduced to through Jeff, the builder. Gerard is building six-plexes in Halifax, and it was not long before Ben was asking him to build two for him so that he could have another 12-plex underway. Ben worked on getting financing through another relationship that he has with a national finance company, and he already had a discussion letter ready for the build with an excellent low-interest rate. The difficulty became the amount of down payment that would be needed. It would probably be about $525,000. And very quickly, Ben asked me if I would be interested in making this investment together so that we would each be responsible for one-half of the down payment.

Having learned so much about the need for rentals in Halifax and reviewing the income numbers that Ben had crunched, it made a lot of sense! So, without hesitation, I said, "Yes, let's do it!"

Ben started to work out the details and put the floor plans together for the build. As this was coming together, we made a couple more trips to Halifax, Nova Scotia, to meet with Gerard and his Mortgage agent, Glen Estabrooks, from The Mortgage Group. These brainstorming meetings resulted in us deciding that we should be the builder ourselves and contract Gerard rather than have him be the builder, and then have us buy it.

The reason behind this thinking was that it is way easier to get a construction mortgage as the builder rather than an ownership mortgage as the buyer. Now we are talking! A good deal just turned into a great deal! Now we can buy it with minimal upfront funds. Even the investor who owns the lots will wait for full payment after the construction is complete, the units are rented, and the final financing is completed. Wow, what a great turn of events.

Now Ben could probably build this even without my financial help. Yet, Ben is a man of his word! We agreed to do the building together, and he has kept that promise, and we have a company together now that will own these two six-plexes that were soon to be built.

In our most recent trip to Halifax to meet again with the builder, we also met with the designer to work out the floor plan details. The most popular floor plan and the one that would bring in the most rent would be a modern concept layout.

During our discussions, we talked about whether the building would be on grade or sunk about four-feet into the grade. Suddenly, these gentlemen who understand construction in Halifax and the municipality rules realized that if we sink it into the grade that we can then add another story and have an eight-plex for a mere $100,000 more. This would mean these extra two units on each building would cost only $50,000 each and add an additional value of $205,000 each!

Now the great deal just became Fabulous! We should be able to build this and pull out $200,000 each when it has the final financing. And each building should have a positive cash flow of $5,000 each month!

All of this has happened because of the great relationships we built with the builders. And the excellent relationship that Ben and I made with each other! Just this past year, Ben decided to come and work with me on my real estate team due to our ongoing excellent friendship.

By the way, Ben is only 31-years-old, and this is only one of the developments that he has on the go. He is still planning to own a tropical island in the future!

It is by pure accident that Ben and I met that day at the TD bank and now only a few years later, we are helping each other become multi-millionaires through real estate ownership. Again, all of these opportunities have come from building relationships. I'm always trying to see how I can help people do more. I've found that building with others has made my life more enjoyable. With complementary skills and attitudes, we can reach goals together. So, when someone you trust says to you, why don't you look at this opportunity. Then take the time and go ahead and look at it! If it seems to be right, then jump in!

Two quotes I live by:

Your attitude will affect your altitude!

Attitude gives the result to your altitude.

This is where mindset comes into play again. I chose to ask Ben to work with me. I decided to tag along to Liverpool, Nova Scotia. I choose to make these decisions, just like I choose to create my moods, which has created a mind for success. You are happy the moment you decide to be happy! People brought me opportunities because I was always positive in attitude. This last story of my support and excitement for Ben May's progress shows just that.

I give off energy rather than take from people. My daily greeting to others is: how are you doing? My good friend, Thomas Wong, always says super fantastic! I always say, Fabbbbbbullllous! And EX-cellent! People simply want to talk with me because of that and the opportunities that only come along from talking with others.

In today's society, many people would rather text than email and maybe even talk on the phone rather than meeting in person. From all of the times that we went to Halifax to meet the builders, it became clear to me that there is nothing better than the face to face meetings. This is how you can have the best communication and collaboration. And those things can lead you to become an accidental millionaire.

When you hang with the right people (that means people that are successful at what you want to do and the people that are thinking bigger than you can at the time) you will grow your opportunities almost by accident, just by putting yourself in the way of opportunity.

Now, you still have to take action when the opportunity is presented to you. And this means taking risks.

Make these calculated risks. Do not blindly commit without first reviewing the numbers and the intangibles that will affect you. And once you realize that you can live with the risk, commit to action and move forward.

Avoid getting into analysis paralysis in waiting for the perfect deal with no risk. That probably does not exist, and if you ever do find it, it will be years later, and you will have missed many valuable money-making opportunities.

I have two clients who went golfing with one of my first investor clients. In comparing their lives while golfing, all three men found that they were doing very well. My investor seemed to be enjoying his situation more. He explained how ten years earlier he had purchased four rental properties with me and how they have paid off for him over the years. He also talked about how the boat that he currently keeps at Cole Harbour in Vancouver had been a direct result of those investments. This is my same friend, Toby Struewing, who also suggested I start doing property management in my business.

After this weekend of golf, both men called me to tell me that they wanted to meet to talk about investing in real estate. One invested almost immediately as there was a condo for sale in his building and managing that as a rental would be so easy. We got this unit under contract, and it is now rented out for better numbers than we had calculated, and this investor is now ready for another unit.

The other golfer met with me and reviewed some options. He is still reviewing them at this time—ten months later. Now, his situation is different and he may take some other things into consideration, yet the longer he waits, the higher the prices go on real estate in our Kitchener-Waterloo area.

I will ask him again for some action to help him along his way to long term wealth building.

It may have been by pure coincidence that these gentlemen all decided to get together to play golf while Toby was visiting Ontario and, again, a coincidence that the topic of wealth and success come up. Yet, without taking action after hearing about the real estate investment opportunity, it would have just been another game of golf instead of a life-changing gamble.

Great Relationships Bring you Great Luck!

Benjamin May in Liverpool, Nova Scotia.

Chapter Twelve

Evolution:
My Advice to The Next Generation

Real estate, it's been around as long as our country, Canada, itself. If you're looking to get involved in real estate, you'll need to understand the different types of property you can invest in and how things have evolved throughout time. Real estate can be residential, rural, commercial, or industrial. Below, I'll give you some basic examples to get your head in the game.

Here are some examples of residential real estate:

- houses
- multiplexes
- condos

Examples of rural real estate:

- ranches
- farms

Examples of commercial real estate:

- shopping centres
- offices
- apartments

Examples of institutional real estate:

- churches
- schools
- hospitals

In the beginning, real estate was a lot more complicated than it is now because of all of our communication tools. Back in the day, we used pagers and spent more time in the office so we could use the phone. Now, it's easier with cell phones, electronic signing, and emails. We can now communicate, travel, and get the job done in this new world, with a lot more ease.

Michelle always says, "Every year is like one-hundred years in technology." And, she's right. That's why it's essential to keep up with the times. It's all about marketing and sales. You have to be great on the phone. The moment you get someone on the line, make it your mission to get them in front of you (in person). Start the fact-finding process immediately.

It's crucial to convert each lead. If you don't look after leads, it's like burning money in your backyard, as Michelle would say. Often, people are all about chasing the next dollar instead of taking care of the people in their backdoor, not realizing that if they take care of those people, the money will multiply!

We have an internal marketing engine and an internal marketing team. That's right, you don't have to be a broker-owner to make money. It's all about the right specialized knowledge and application of that knowledge to help people.

My advice to the next generation of agents and brokers:

To become successful in real estate, make sure everyone knows you're in the game. Make sure your clients remember you are excellent at what you do and look out for the client's best interest at all times. Deliver on your promises and leverage it. One must ask for referrals. I've always taken great pride in being at the top in referrals.

When you ask for referrals, your clientele will skyrocket.

Follow up on your past clients and build life-long relationships with each person you get the privilege to work alongside. Building relationships will set you apart from the average real estate professional because when you nurture your past clients, it leads to long-standing loyalty and more sales in the future through positive word of mouth.

Seeing other people happy makes me happy. I'm continually looking for ways to help others, listening actively, and questioning each client three-deep. If someone says to you, they are looking for a big yard, you say, "tell me more." If they say they need it to be fifty-feet, you ask, "why is that?" From there, you may determine that they are planning on putting in a pool, and you continue to gather info to make sure you have the right size and layout in mind. Questioning three-deep allows you to make things clear. You begin to understand what the client is looking for in full detail. This strategy will bring results and ensure the client is getting everything they imagined, and more.

Chapter Thirteen

More Lessons in Real Estate

The Millionaire Real Estate Investor Seminar:

This seminar got me fired up, and I've been to a lot of different investor seminars. I was already investing in properties. Keller Williams sponsored the investors' workshop, in particular by Jeff Reitzel. I have to say if you have never attended an investor seminar, I strongly suggest you try one. The amount of knowledge that floats around at one of these events, you will never learn anywhere else. This one was one of the most powerful ones I've been to, in fact, so powerful, afterward, I went out and bought a brand-new house. This was the seminar where I had decided to keep my rental properties long-term instead of for the short time I had been doing. I let them be a wealth creation for my family and me.

Because of this seminar, I re-structured my investing strategy entirely.

West Meadow Drive, Kitchener:

So, after the investors seminar, I went out the very next day and bought a brand-new build by East Forest Homes, it was on West Meadow Drive in Kitchener. I was still a bit timid about rentals due to the awful experience I had with my first investment on London Road in Guelph where I put in really bad tenants. This time, I was buying a brand-new building and I didn't know who I was going to have as a tenant. At this point, I didn't have much experience with rental properties, so I was learning as I went along, it's all about the mindset, right?

I got this brand-new house, so I put an ad up on Kijiji, and to my surprise, I had a response super-fast, within minutes, and to my relief, it was a woman I knew. She was well known in the real estate field. Her name is Denise. She is an awesome Real Estate Agent, and I liked her, and I thought perfect, she would make a fantastic tenant. So, I called her.

Once I had connected with Denise, I mentioned to her that it was my house. There was a sigh of relief on the phone from her as she said, "Oh, thank God Roy, I was afraid I was going to end up with a creep as a landlord," which is a true worry when you're a beautiful lady. You can get some creeps out there, right? I said to her, "Well, thank God, it's you because I was afraid, I was going to get a creep of a tenant."

We both laughed.

She was the best tenant I have ever had; she kept the house spotless and beautiful. She would often have Nikki and me over, at least twice a year, to see the house. I remember saying to Nikki, that that house was nicer than ours because it was so new. Everything was still clean with no chips in the baseboards and no walls that needed repainting. I think we were just about to repaint our home. It needed to have a fresh look. Our place had two growing boys living there, and we all know what boys are like sometimes.

Denise was renting from me for about two years when she had approached me to buy the house. I threw my hands up, waving no, no, no, I bought this house to keep forever and to pass it down through the family. So, I don't want to sell it.

I said to her, "Go buy another house, Denise!"

She laughed at me and said, "Oh no, Roy, you have to sell me this house. I've been here since it was brand new, and I have looked after it all this time. I want this to continue to be my home."

I still said no, shaking my head.

I was so bloody determined to keep that house as a rental.

She left in a huff, and I thought that it was the end of our conversation. Well, now, I know why. Denise was such a great agent. I laughed because when I got home, I walked in and saw Nikki standing there with her arms crossed with that look on her face. Yes, all you married guys know exactly which look I'm talking about.

I found out that Denise had called my wife, and they had a chat. I knew right away that I lost that one. I called Denise and said, "Okay you both beat me into submission, I give up, I'll sell it to you." That's okay, I was actually thinking about buying a home in Florida for retirement, and this worked out well because it had freed up funds to do just that. See, mindset always prevails. So, we bought our first home in Florida after we sold the house to Denise.

The Florida house that I found was on sale now due to the market crash, so it went from $250,000 a few years earlier to $80,000. The dollar was at par, so we bought it! And then each of the next two years, I bought another home in Florida at the same price point, $80,000 each. And to this day, those three USA homes are some of my best cash flow because of the exchange rate between the US and Canadian dollar.

The Canadian Property Bubble:

Here is a little history for you on the Canadian property bubble…

It's the rise in Canadian real estate prices, starting in 2003 and is still going on today. During this period, homes and property prices have increased by up to 337% in some cities in Canada. The real estate world describes this as a bubble. In 2018, the cost of owning a home was above the levels in the early 90s when Canadians experienced its previous housing bubble burst!

In 2010, foreign investment caused a boom in the real estate marketplace, which led to a major price increase in not only owning a home but renting a home as well. A fall in interest rates, combined with a rise in home prices since the 90s, told the buyers and renters that the market was stable for long-term investments.

Even though the supply of homes was limited, it brought more buyers into the market, but they were cautious. First time home buyers started to see the value of owning a home, but they were struggling to find one at a reasonable price. In 2017, the housing market in the greater Toronto area saw increases of 33% in just one year. More than half of that (19%), was in the last two months of that year.

Even in the less sought after duplexes, it has increased to over a million dollars. Outside of the GTA saw price increases too. Dilapidated homes were selling way over the asking price. Condo construction saw consistent growth with each passing year, even while under construction.

Due to the high increases, in such a short period of time, it caused great panic. Everyone was scrambling because they had never seen such a massive spike like that in their lives. The government attempted to step in to help regulate in slowing down the high prices by bringing down the prices naturally.

There were so many homes on the market, with no buyers. People couldn't afford these new prices. Thus, the government tried to bring down the costs to assist first time home buyers in helping prevent a crash.

In April of 2017, the Canadian Federal Finance Minister, Bill Morneau, met with Charles Sousa and John Tory to find a resolution. From this meeting, their solution was to implement a foreign buyer tax and speculation tax — also, a provincial fair housing plan to control rent.

Insured buyers were put through a stress test to see if they were up for handling the rising rates. The three solutions that were put in place are the cause of the slight drop in housing prices.

A Fair Housing Plan was created, with sixteen points. Here are the points:

1. Non-resident speculation tax

2. Rent is only allowed to rise at rates posted in the annual provincial rental increase guideline

3. Develop standard leases that would further help protect tenants and ensure landlords

4. Create a program to balance the value of surplus land assets

5. Put a vacant property tax into place

6. Tax to make sure new apartment complexes is similar to other current complex properties

7. Introduce a five-year program to facilitate the building of more rental apartments

8. Make it easier to use property taxes to generate more development opportunities

9. Create a housing supply team to help uncover and fix barriers to housing developments

10. Work to fight tax avoidance practices

11. Releases rules involving customer representation in real estate transactions

12. Creation of a housing group to advise the government about what is happening in the housing market

13. More education for consumers about their real estate rates

14. Create more through reporting requirements for real estate sales

15. Improve reliability of elevators in Ontario buildings

16. Updating the Growth Plan for the Greater Golden Horseshoe

What's happening now?

As I write this book, we are in the middle of a lockdown to quarantine the public against COVID-19. This is causing an incredible shock to the economy and we really do not know how this will affect home prices for the balance of 2020 or the years beyond. At the same time in Alberta, they are in a recession with high unemployment due to the low price of oil causing a lack of new investment in the province. This is due to the oil-producing countries no longer agreeing to limit the amount of oil being produced each day. Mortgage rates continue to fluctuate with the economy, and owning a home has started to cost more than 50% of the

household's income.

In short, Canada's housing market is very much in uncharted territory. We don't know what's going to happen, but we are desperately trying to fix it. Our wages aren't going up to pay for the increased housing market. So, as much as they are trying to make it easier, it isn't. This is one of the very reasons why I have always focused on rent-to-owns to try and make it more affordable for my clients. I want to help people get into a home sooner rather than later. When you are renting, you are still paying a mortgage, it just so happens to be the landlord's mortgage instead of your own mortgage.

Chapter Fourteen

The Best is Yet to Come

In real estate, I hope that I can continue to provide people with beautiful affordable housing as rentals, as well as keep creating the possibility for more solutions in the struggle to find the right home and live a comfortable life, as we all deserve. As for my partnerships, I will continue to give Michelle freedom and support; she has been and will continue to be a fantastic asset. My main goal is always to support my business partner and team.

I believe in paying it forward and will continue to pioneer in ways to give back, helping more and more people in ways that I can. With a considerable amount of gratitude, I realize the importance of giving back. My goal for the business is to accumulate 100 million in sales commission in ten years. We will do that by continuing to build our team and our services.

> "Money is good for the good you can do with the money."
> - Jeff Reitzel

> "By helping others, I help myself."
> - unknown

> "If you aren't doing anything, nothing will happen. If you're doing something, then something will happen."
> - Roy Cleeves

Closing the video store was one of my biggest struggles. It was the bottom, like starting from scratch. But even though the store didn't work out, I knew something else would come along and work out. Everything happens for a reason, always have faith! Like the property, I bought with Chris with the horrible tenants. We had to evict and rebuild and look where that took us. I ended up doing twenty-five deals in half a year, with enough money to spoil Nikki with the Mustang Convertible that she always wanted. Like my dad always taught me, things will work out, so don't worry and put in the work.

I knew I would make it big one day! Maybe I didn't know exactly how it would all unfold, and I definitely wasn't expecting my first year in real estate to take off as it did, but I was always optimistic. And, after I hit it big, I continued to grow. If you surround yourself with the right people and take action on opportunities presented to you, you can become an accidental millionaire too!

> "Make a million or die trying."
> -Roy Cleeves

I have always envisioned myself in a sea of money!

Chapter Fifteen

Afterthoughts

In the end, real estate goes up in value in the long-term. It's an excellent investment that everyone should try to do, even if it's just a home to live your life!

One of the best ways to create wealth is to INVEST in real estate. It can change your life for the better and create a legacy for your family and the generations to come.

This book was created to inspire people of all backgrounds to make smart investments in their lives. The right investment can lead to growth beyond your wildest dreams. I've made a living from investing and this book is just the tip of how I started. My next goal is to share the model with people interested in taking it further.

> **"If I can do it, then you can do it too."**
> **-unknown**

Epilogue

In January 2020, I, along with Nikki, our good friends and investment partners, Scott and Pauline, went on a trip to the South China Seas. This trip took us from Hong Kong to Singapore to Thailand to Cambodia to Vietnam and then back to Hong Kong, followed by a long flight home to Canada.

We returned to Toronto, Canada on the 26th day of January, and at that time, there was talk of the Coronavirus spreading in Wuhan, China. As we travelled through the Hong Kong airport, the security guards checked us for our temperature to ensure we were not showing any signs of the virus. We returned home on a full flight and little did we know that that would be the last flight for a long time due to the social distancing that will soon be part of our normal life after COVID-19 came to Canada.

In terms of real estate, it was looking like 2020 would be one of our biggest years yet, with record sales in January and February and even the first half of March until the Canadian government locked down the travel of people and the closure of many businesses. Most all of the deals that were already done and waiting to close still ended up closing with the odd exception, yet mostly everyone was able to close.

There are cases where people decided to stop looking, and people decided to stop putting their home on the market until the COVID-19 state of emergency was over. It's still not over yet, so pent-up supply and pent-up demand will be available once COVID-19 is curtailed.

Sales in March ended up relatively stable still since the first half of the month was strong before the lockdown was ordered. Sales numbers in April had declined by 63% compared to the same month in the previous year. The interesting thing is that supply and demand retreated at the same time and at the same level such that the prices remain stable and even growing. Prices actually climbed in our market by 7% in April 2020 compared to April 2019.

There was a lot of worry about whether or not tenants would pay the rent due in April 2020 since the government said to the tenants and people renting that if it is between rent and food to choose food. And the only form of control that we have over tenants is really the landlord-tenant board hearings for when a tenant does not pay the rent, and these were all closed as part of the government closures to stop the spread of the virus.

It is at a time like this; you will find out how well you have done to select tenants for your rental properties. We have been very fortunate that we have selected excellent tenants. We have treated them well, and in turn, they have treated us well. They have paid their rent not only for April 2020 but also for May 2020 and June 2020.

I even have one tenant that sent me the following texts:

"Hi, Roy. I was wondering something. We all work in essential jobs, which is good; however, if one of us gets exposed, we would all be off work for 14 days. Are you fine with me paying April and May rent now, so I don't have to worry about anything for the next two months."

"I will go ahead and send that and make an effort to get June rent paid by early to mid-May as that may help you out if you have any other renters that have trouble paying their rent."

This is an excellent tenant, and of course, I know them well. They have been paying well for probably seven years in that house. As an investor, it is always good to have a three month supply of emergency funds in the bank to handle any surprises like this pandemic.

Also, during this time, I had a couple of tenants that decided to give notice and leave their rental, which meant we needed to advertise and find new tenants. In both cases, we ended up with tenants that were referred to us by existing clients. It made it a lot easier for our new tenants to move in and for our existing tenants to move out.

We learn to adapt the way that we work to do things online and with social distancing to ensure the health and safety of everyone and to flatten the curve on the spread of the COVID-19. The question is, how will the economic shutdown and the loss of so many jobs affect the price of real estate, the business of real estate, and the rentals' expense in the market?

We are not out of it yet! As I am writing this, we cannot predict exactly what will happen as we have never seen this before. However, rental and house pricing has remained steady. The volume has fallen in the business of sales and rentals yet still allowed us to survive.

Being the positive people we are, we have been able to keep the team very happy and healthy during this time. They are all looking forward to the pent-up demand of greater business as things ease up, and more people put their homes on the market and get out to see homes to buy.

The COVID-19 pandemic has affected everyone, at least in some way. So many people had to cancel the trips they had planned. Many people had to cancel get-togethers and celebrations such as graduation, birthdays, weddings, anniversaries, and so much more. On top of that, the very large public gatherings such as rock concerts, sports games, and business conventions have all been cancelled without an exact revival date.

During the pandemic, two of my friends each had their mother passed away. One friend decided that they would do a celebration of life when the gatherings allowed. In the meantime, the ashes are being stored for the celebration. My other friend decided to continue with the regular funeral through the funeral home. The funeral home did social distancing at the funeral parlour, and my friend set up his laptop and did a zoom link for all of us to attend.

The amazing thing about using Zoom and online digitally was that it allowed people from all over the world to attend the funeral, who otherwise would not have been able to attend in any fashion.

With so many businesses having to conduct online, I predict that when social gatherings are allowed again, there will probably be a hybrid of these two systems, allowing people to connect digitally when it works best for them and to connect in person when possible.

Gary Keller of Keller Williams Realty has said, going forward, our businesses will be digital and physically enhanced rather than the other way around. To look after our clients, the very best way that we can, it is great to start digitally, especially where we can see each other on the zoom link or some similar media and then do follow up with meetings in person. There is no better way to have a clear understanding of your client's wants and needs than communicating in person. In-person allows us to read body language that you cannot always see in a video link.

The pandemic and the ensuing state of emergency have created kindness in us all to care and look after our fellow human beings, including our tenants, our work families, and our home families.

I found that we have all become more patient. We are now willing to wait in line to get into a store. It has removed a lot of the things that we took for granted and now makes us appreciate a lot of our everyday conveniences. Without a doubt, the number one lesson that this pandemic has taught us is to stay safe and look after each other.

So, on that note, I wish you all to **stay safe and take care of one another.**

ACKNOWLEDGMENTS

Special Thanks

To my wife, Nikki, and my Sons, Skyler and Jagger, for showing me unconditional love and support throughout my journey.

To my parents, Penny and Mel for teaching me my gut values and for always supporting me in my business ventures.

To my Business Partner & Brother-in-Law, Chris Abbott, who motivated me to invest in Real Estate and to become a REALTOR®.

To my Business Partner and Financier, Thomas Wong, for teaching me a rent-to-own investment strategy and helping me along the way with investment funds.

To my Business Partners and Travel Partners, Scott Harris, and Pauline Delaney, for investing with Nikki and me and for all of the most excellent travel vacations that we have taken together.

To my Business Partner, Benjamin May, for taking me to Nova Scotia to invest with him in his projects there.

To my Business Partner, David Anderson, for working with me for so many years right from when we were both newer agents.

To my Business Partner, Michelle Carty, for growing our team in Burlington and for encouraging me to take the plunge to write this book.

To my Team Mates at Keller Williams Realty for their hard work and support and training in helping me run a successful business that led me to this venture.

To all of my Friends and Clients that have referred business and opportunities to me and for all of the business that we have done together over the years.

To the Reitzel Family who owns Keller Williams Golden Triangle Realty and Mortgage Alliance Canada's Mortgage Choice, for all of your support of me and my team.

To Roy Singh, who owned Century 21 Home Realty, for inviting me to work at your Brokerage when I was brand new and for sharing your training and experience. And for laying out a plan on investing that sat in my mind for years.

To The Optimist Club of Stanley Park for your support and guidance with the Optimist Creed.

To my editor, Linsey Fischer, for her hard work putting together my book with me. Thank you, Rayko, for his input on the project. To Gordon So, for painting a vision and making this project possible.

Author's Bio

**Author:
Roy Cleeves, Real Estate Broker, Agent, Investor, &
Businessman.**

Roy has an Honours in Bachelor of Business Administration. He is a graduate of Wilfrid Laurier University. Roy invests in various Real Estate Projects including an amazing rent-to-own program. At present, his real estate holding exceeds 18 properties, including three in the Orlando area of Florida, USA.

As a Real Estate Investor, Roy realized that he should know even more about the process of buying and selling real estate, so it was only natural for Roy to become a REALTOR®. as this is his passion!

Now the CC Realty Group is one of the top teams in all of Keller Williams Canada Brokerages and specifically at Keller Williams Golden Triangle Realty and Keller Williams Edge Realty.

What does the CC Realty Group do differently from every other REALTOR® out there?

1. Clients are getting the power of a Team for the same investment (if you are selling) as a single agent. And if you are a buyer this means that the team always ensures someone is available to show you homes that will fit your schedule.

2. The Team has a dedicated Operations Coordinator, John Dewar. For sellers, this means that showings are always a priority and booked appropriately as per the seller's wishes. John ensures all interested REALTOR®'s are advised, as an offer comes in, to ensure that every opportunity, for a Multiple offer, is given to our sellers. And for buyers, John ensures that all of the conditions of the purchase are followed up on and that all of the paperwork needed for the lawyer's office is complete.

3. Constant communication with Clients and prospects and all REALTOR®'s in the region to maximize exposure of your home when for sale and to learn of excellent buying opportunities, including exclusive listings, power of sales, and company sales.

4. EXPERIENCE – Since 2003, Roy and his team have assisted in the transaction of over 1,500 homes and have gone through some unusual situations – enough to write another book! This

Experience is key to getting the Buyer and Seller together to complete the transaction.

5. The Team is always implementing new Marketing Techniques. The latest are REVERSE OFFERS, IDX WEBSITES, ALL SOCIAL MEDIA, GUARANTEED SALE PROGRAM, and RENT-TO- OWN.

6. The Team has a network of associates for all of the Sub Trade work that you may need for your home and all of these associates are trusted by the CC Realty Group. They are always great value for their services.

7. Passion and Commitment. Roy and the Team are passionate about Real Estate and Committed to you! This is our FULL-TIME CAREER and not just a part time job.

8. Superior Communication Standards. The Team is always available by TEXT, CELL, EMAIL, MESSENGER to SMART PHONES and Desktops/laptops/ipads. And the Team always has someone available all days including Weekends and Holidays.

9. Family Values! We believe in Family First! We place HONESTY, TRUST & INTEGRITY above all else! Our Reputation precedes us.

10. Our Mission: We strive to be your Real Estate Consultants for Life!

Contact Roy at any time. He is ALWAYS ready to talk about Real Estate, and he is always looking for new people to invest with!

roy@ccrealtygroup.ca

Editor's Bio

Linsey Fischer is an Editor and Writing Coach. She has coached over one hundred aspiring authors to share their message through writing. Linsey has a background in both print and broadcast journalism. She got her professional start as a writer at the age of 17, writing a weekly column in her hometown newspaper: The Brantford Expositor. She went on to get her post-secondary education in Broadcast Journalism, where she developed the skills to hone in on important subjects and bring the magic to light through reporting and spotlight stories on radio and television. Today, Linsey has worked on a variety of different book series and has won an award for the work she did on the *Empowering Women to Succeed* series. Linsey has also co-authored a number of #1 international best selling books on Amazon and has new books coming out in the next few years. Follow her on social media for updates.

RESOURCES

1. Luck, Marissa (4 May 2018). "Keller Williams' growing army of agents eclipses most cities' populations". Austin Business Journal. Retrieved 11 June 2018.

2. Sullivan, Marilyn D. (2006). The Complete Idiot's Guide to Success as a Real Estate Agent. Penguin. ISBN 9781592575657.

3. Weingartner, Nancy (1999). "Keller Williams has sales associates dive into the profit-sharing pool". Franchise Times.

4. Simmons, Lee (24 May 1998). "Realtor saw opportunity in adversity". Austin Business Journal. Retrieved 19 May 2014.

5. Pleasant, Rachel (10 September 2003). "New Realty Goes for Brokers". Lakeland Ledger. Retrieved 19 May 2014.

6. ^ Vyas, Charul (16 November 1997). "Success finds Keller Williams, Schlotzskys". Austin Business Journal. Retrieved 19 May 2014.

7. Martin, Joan (18 September 2004). "With 114 Realtors, Keller Williams Realty is now biggest real estate firm in Polk County". Lakeland Ledger. Retrieved 19 May 2014.

8. ^ Martin, Joan (19 June 2004). "Keller Williams Takes Off All Over Florida". Lakeland Ledger. Retrieved 19 May 2014.

9. ^ "Keller Williams Realty Announces Luxury Homes Program – Opens doors to high-end market in Saint Louis MO". St. Louis Real Estate Today. 12 September 2007. Retrieved 19 May 2014.

10. Cronan, Carl (18 June 2007). "Keller Williams expands into commercial arena, taps agents for leads". Tampa Bay Business Journal. Retrieved 19 May 2014.

11. "Jeff Rohn Named Managing Director of the KW Commercial Peninsula Office". The Registry. 4 June 2012. Retrieved 19 May 2014.

12. Egan, John (8 March 2001). "Austin's Keller Williams targets global expansion". The Examiner.

13. Garrison, Trey (18 February 2014). "Keller Williams posts major growth, plans Dubai office". Housing Wire. Retrieved 19 May 2014.

14. "Keller Williams tops 100K agents worldwide". Inman. 7 May 2014. Retrieved 19 May 2014.

15. Buchholz, Jan (8 May 2014). "Keller Williams hits milestone with 100,575 agents worldwide". Austin Business Journal. Retrieved 16 May 2014.

16. Gupta, Rapti (18 February 2013). "Keller Williams Realty Ranked #1 by Agent Count in US". Realty Today. Retrieved 19 May 2014.

17. Hunt, Angela (15 April 2014). "Keller Williams taps Manhattan exec to run operation in Dubai". The Real Deal. Retrieved 19 May 2014.

18. Sambidge, Andy (14 April 2014). "Largest US real estate franchise to launch ops in Dubai". Arabian Business. Retrieved 19 May 2014.

19. Taufen, Amber (19 January 2017). "Keller Williams agents grew sales volume by 22% in 2016". Inman. Retrieved 11 June 2018.

20. Abraham, Rincey (1 March 2018). "Keller Williams Hopes to Become the Amazon of Real Estate". Miami Agent Magazine. Retrieved 11 June 2018.

21. Solomont, E.B. (31 January 2018). "Keller Williams claims it's now the No. 1 franchise in the US". The Real Deal. Retrieved 15 June 2018.

22. Bondarenko, Veronika (5 April 2018). "Keller Williams continues South America expansion with new Argentina branch". Inman. Retrieved 20 June 2018.

23. McPherson, Marian (30 August 2018). "Keller Williams heads to Cambodia". Inman. Retrieved 20 July 2019.

24. "Gary Keller returns as CEO of nation's largest realty company". Austin Business Journal. 9 January 2019. Retrieved 9 January 2019.

25. "Next stop for Keller Williams? Morocco". The Real Deal. 4 June 2019. Retrieved 21 July 2019.

26. Sain, Cliff (22 April 2014). "More than 200 take part in inaugural 5K". Branson Tri Lake News. Retrieved 19 May 2014.

27. "What We Do". KW Cares. Retrieved 19 May 2014.

28. Baron, Sharon Aron (12 May 2014). "Local Business Shuts Down for a Worthy Community Project". Tamarac Talk. Retrieved 19 May 2014.

29. "Keller Williams employees give back, work hard on RED day". The Montgomery County Courier. 11 May 2014. Retrieved 19 May 2014.

30. ^ "Keller Williams marks RED Day with service to SCHFH". Cape Gazette. 13 May 2014. Retrieved 19 May 2014.

31. "Keller Williams Realty". Inc. Magazine. Retrieved 19 May 2014.

32. Herold, Tracy Stapp (22 April 2011). "Entrepreneur's 2011 Best of the Best Franchises List". Entrepreneur Magazine. Retrieved 19 May 2014.

33. Kearns, Patrick (17 January 2018). "Which real estate companies made the 2018 Franchise 500 cut?". Inman. Retrieved 15 June 2018.

34. South, Gill (14 February 2018). "LeadingRE ranks first on 'Training' Top 125, Keller Williams inducted into Hall of Fame". Inman. Retrieved 15 June 2018.

35. Kauflin, Jeff (3 December 2017). "The Happiest Companies to Work for in 2018".

36. Haber, Bob. "Canadian Real Estate Bubble Blowing Up North." Forbes, Forbes Magazine, 3 Apr. 2018, www.forbes.com/sites/bobhaber/2018/04/02/canadian-real-estate-bubble-blowing-up-north/#1b74d3871d5e.

37. Tencer, Daniel (3 October 2018). Canada At Risk As 'First Cracks' Appear In Global Housing Bubbles: UBS., HuffPost (Canada edition)

38. Castaldo, Joe. "How Canada's Real Estate Market Went Completely Insane." Canadian Business - Your Source For Business News, 10 July 2017, www.canadianbusiness.com/economy/how-canadas-real-estate-market-went-completely-insane/.

39. Castaldo, Joe. "How Canada's Real Estate Market Went Completely Insane." Canadian Business - Your Source For Business News, 10 July 2017, www.canadianbusiness.com/economy/how-canadas-real-estate-market-went-completely-insane/.

40. Castaldo, Joe. "How Canada's Real Estate Market Went Completely Insane." Canadian Business - Your Source For Business News, 10 July 2017, www.canadianbusiness.com/economy/how-canadas-real-estate-market-went-completely-insane/.

41. Andrews, Jeff. "Canada's Housing Bubble Is Starting to Burst." Curbed, Curbed, 7 Mar. 2018, www.curbed.com/2018/3/7/17085794/canada-housing-market-collapse.

42. Tencer, Daniel. "Canada At Risk As 'First Cracks' Appear In Global Housing Bubbles: UBS." HuffPost Canada, HuffPost Canada, 3 Oct. 2018, www.huffingtonpost.ca/2018/09/29/

toronto-vancouver-have-world-s-3rd-and-4th-largest-housing-bubbles-ubs_a_23544956/.

43. Andrews, Jeff. "Canada's Housing Bubble Is Starting to Burst." Curbed, Curbed, 7 Mar. 2018, www.curbed.com/2018/3/7/17085794/canada-housing-market-collapse.

44. "Ontario's Fair Housing Plan." News.ontario.ca, news.ontario.ca/mof/en/2017/04/ontarios-fair-housing-plan.html.

45. Haber, Bob. "Canadian Real Estate Bubble Blowing Up North." Forbes, Forbes Magazine, 3 Apr. 2018, www.forbes.com/sites/bobhaber/2018/04/02/canadian-real-estate-bubble-blowing-up-north/#1b74d3871d5e.

46. Castaldo, Joe. "How Canada's Real Estate Market Went Completely Insane." Canadian Business - Your Source For Business News, 10 July 2017, www.canadianbusiness.com/economy/how-canadas-real-estate-market-went-completely-insane/.

47. Tencer, Daniel. "Canada At Risk As 'First Cracks' Appear In Global Housing Bubbles: UBS." HuffPost Canada, HuffPost Canada, 3 Oct. 2018, www.huffingtonpost.ca/2018/09/29/toronto-vancouver-have-world-s-3rd-and-4th-largest-housing-bubbles-ubs_a_23544956/.

48. Andrews, Jeff. "Canada's Housing Bubble Is Starting to Burst." Curbed, Curbed, 7 Mar. 2018, www.curbed.com/2018/3/7/17085794/canada-housing-market-collapse.

49. "Canada's Housing Market Still 'Highly Vulnerable' despite Easing Prices, CMHC Warns." Financial Post, 25 Oct. 2018, business.financialpost.com/real-estate/prices-easing-but-canadas-housing-market-still-highly-vulnerable-cmhc.

50. Alini, Erica. "Will It Crash? Here's What to Expect from the Canadian Housing Market in 2019." Global News, Global News, 2 Dec. 2018, globalnews.ca/news/4688308/canada-housing-market-outlook-2019/.

51. Khan, Mikael (April 2019). "Disentangling the Factors Driving Housing Resales" (PDF). Bank of Canada. p. 8. Retrieved 13 May 2019.

52. Castaldo, Joe. "How Canada's Real Estate Market Went Completely Insane." Canadian Business - Your Source For Business News, 10 July 2017, www.canadianbusiness.com/economy/how-canadas-real-estate-market-went-completely-insane/.

53. Andrews, Jeff. "Canada's Housing Bubble Is Starting to Burst." Curbed, Curbed, 7 Mar. 2018, www.curbed.com/2018/3/7/17085794/canada-housing-market-collapse.

54. Castaldo, Joe. "How Canada's Real Estate Market Went Completely Insane." Canadian Business - Your Source For Business News, 10 July 2017, www.canadianbusiness.com/economy/how-canadas-real-estate-market-went-completely-insane/

55. kw.com

www.ingramcontent.com/pod-product-compliance
Lightning Source LLC
Chambersburg PA
CBHW060850220526
45466CB00003B/1316